CRESCENDO

ANTHEA KRESTON

CRESCENDO

Chronicles of an Adventurous Violinist

pdb

PAUL DRY BOOKS
Philadelphia 2026

First Paul Dry Books Edition, 2026

Paul Dry Books, Inc.
Philadelphia, Pennsylvania
www.pauldrybooks.com

Photo on p. 190 taken by Erika Nagamoto

Printed in the United States of America

Library of Congress Control Number: 2026944784

ISBN: 978-1-58988-217-1

To my husband, Jason,
and our daughters, Mirabai and Tzippora.
It's been quite an adventure so far.

Contents

1
Vortex

It's easy to lose yourself in a string quartet, to lose family, friends, your own life.

I know this too sharply, with too much clarity. Someone actually had to die for me to be here. I am the replacement for a quartet member who took their own life after one of these long tours. They'd had enough. *And I get it.* I get *why.*

I breathe as one with the three other musicians under the white-hot stage lights. We are close enough to touch one another, to smell each other; the sweetness of our commingled sweat, the bitterness of sharply exhaled lungs. Even closer to me, held firmly between collarbone and chin, as much a part of my body as my arms, my heart, my violin speaks words that I would never dare to utter. She knows my deepest secrets and desires. My partner for over thirty years. I know every inch of her: her weaknesses and strengths; the grooves worn into the dark, strong wood by my fingers; pale lines across her body etched by my tears of frustration; the scratch left from an exuberant pizzicato revealed under the harsh spotlight. The history of my life is written on her, and *with* her, my future will unfold.

She has not left my side since age fourteen, a posthumous gift from my adored and eccentric grandfather. Stolen and returned, broken and fixed, she has saved me from danger, given me the courage to take enormous chances, has played with Yo-Yo Ma, been played by Isaac Stern. Traveled from Tajikistan to London and myriad points between. She and I are one, and with determination, we tackle life's challenges with humor, tenderness, and brute strength.

Alongside the other members of the Artemis String Quartet, I am poised to begin the first, massive unison melody of Beethoven's earth-shattering *Grosse Fuge*. The four of us look directly into each other's eyes, knowing that once we inhale together, we will be sucked into this dark, violent, and tender world. We freeze, feeling a thousand eyes on us; we are controlling not only ourselves but also the audience. We force the energy of the concert hall to distill and narrow, and as our bows are in the air, frozen, the audience becomes utterly silent.

I can feel the stillness of these strangers, tense and watching, waiting with us as we take this step together. On stage it is more intimate than being with a lover, breathing together, moving together. When we play, the audience recedes and it is only the four of us, immersed in the music.

I am no longer myself, but an embodiment of the desperation of this musical tale, and I see in each of my three colleagues the same commitment, the same determination and intensity.

They demand that I disappear into what we create together, our arms synchronized in large, muscular motions. And I demand it from *them*.

For weeks on end, I lose myself, pushing down my personality in order to meld into this job and what this

German culture expects of me—it's not OK, apparently, to make jokes when you are a member of a serious string quartet. To be a regular person who sometimes (God forbid) makes a mistake, who doesn't craft every single thing that I do or say. Can't I just *be*?

What am I doing here, I wonder, on stage in Amsterdam, New York, Hong Kong, Paris, Berlin? I'm just a normal person, a Midwestern girl who likes to play video games and smoke the occasional doobie. I can recognize my shell; I still look kind of like me, but where are my funky orange bell-bottomed corduroys, my chubby lavender boots? The real me won't fly at the post-concert dinner parties, or even at a rehearsal or going to the grocery store. I have to be "on" for this job. At all times.

I am playing to sold-out audiences, night after night, as a member of one of the best string quartets in the world. It's destroying me as much as it is forcing me to be better than I ever was. And I do neglect my family, inevitably, away on tour for huge stretches of time, my two little kids and my partner staying behind in Berlin, the far-away city where they moved to be with me on this adventure.

𝄐

As the first statement ends, the relentless musical line cuts to a single, fragile melody. Our bodies shaking from exertion, we quiet our beating hearts to now find the calm, lonely music. Our hands vibrate in perfect synchronicity, the chords bending sound to our desires, our intonation choices *physically changing* the length of sound waves. Intoxicating, in the dance between control, exacting unison, and the series of solos which are different every night, night after night.

We are storytellers, living the lives of past geniuses. Beethoven, Shostakovich, Mozart. The struggles and joys that these great masters have written onto parchment come through our arms, our fingers, and our hearts, wrapping in and around the four of us. The tendrils reach out to the mass of strangers in the audience.

The music changes me, lives in my ears all day, inseparable from my life. We are inside a most miraculous work of art; creating a new world; inspiring one another, despite the egos, the tensions and exhaustion. Together, we create something bigger than the four of us, and as we step away from our music stands, thunderous applause filling our ears, four glistening sweat rings on the wooden stage mark our passage together.

Minutes later, with barely a moment to breathe, I am in my dressing room changing out of my drenched concert clothes, and the stage managers whisk us off to sign autographs. Flutes of champagne are set next to our pens on the signing table, lines of fans wrapping around the massive lobby. Then to the after-party, a restaurant opened late just for us, our managers, publicist, presenters, and major supporters along a beautifully laid table. Multiple courses, each paired with a specific wine or liquor, plates set and removed simultaneously, table lit by chandeliers. A collection of languages slide together, toasts are made. Whispery thin, edible gold leaf sits atop the miniature, multilayered chocolate mounds. I never see a price list, a bill.

Off to the hotel, hitting the pillow in the wee hours of the morning after a shower and packing, and up again the same morning at dawn to start the process again, to get into the taxi to the airport and to the next city, to the hotel, to the next stage, to the next Beethoven. We are the Artemis String Quartet, Germany's most celebrated: beloved, wounded, but strong.

This is the best of what it means to be a member of

this world-renowned quartet, as I was from 2016 to 2019. It is at once one of the most extraordinary and most demanding times of my life.

My life, fifty-four years of it so far, has been filled to the brim with adventure, love, loss, and fulfillment. And none of it would have been possible without my violin at my side, giving me the determination to strive for something more, always taking chances and living fully. This is the story of that one true love and our journey together.

※ 2 Calculated Risks

The frigid early morning wind cuts into my face as I stand nervously waiting for a cab to take me to the O'Hare airport in Chicago. I am shivering, not only from the stinging wind but from fear, anticipation, and the tentative bloom of hope that I might be able to begin a new life. The back of my throat is burning; I force bile down by swallowing in short, staccato gulps. I have been throwing up blood pretty regularly for months, almost constant pain from my abdomen to my throat often causing me to double over. A couple of weeks ago my mother had brought me to the emergency room in the middle of the night. My vomiting wouldn't stop and there was more blood than usual. They found a sizable hole in my stomach. I wasn't surprised. My life was eating me from the inside out.

I have an army surplus backpack, my violin, and $437 in cash, dwindled from the $585 I saved from babysitting after paying for the one-way flight to Minneapolis. It's 1989. I am sixteen and I am leaving home.

My parents are vehement. They don't want me to go. They want me to stay and finish high school like the other kids, to take advantage of my excellent school and the many opportunities waiting for me this year. Without their knowledge, I applied for and was admitted to a program for talented youth to start college early, with a full scholarship at the University of Minnesota. My oldest sister (I'm the youngest of three girls) offered me a futon on the floor of the kitchen of her studio apartment for three weeks, enough time for me to either find a job to pay for room and board or to turn around and go back home.

I could have stayed in Chicago, I guess. But everything inside me screamed "go." Screamed and cried and threw up. Waiting for the cab, I clutch my violin to my chest. I draw strength from the beautiful piece of auburn wood. We are partners. This violin is my ticket out, and I know we will make it, together.

She is much more than a finely crafted piece of wood. Through the thousands of hours we have worked together, my confidence has grown. I regularly brave large audiences of critical listeners, throw all of my experiences and emotions into the music, find ways of affecting those strangers in deep, profound ways. I have something to say, something too complex to put into words.

She gives me, after fourteen years of incessant work, a foot in the door of a university that needs a violinist, that needs a leader for their program. Much like sports programs, music departments will search for and recruit strong players, offering them full scholarship in return for the competitions and accolades they expect the student will win while attending their school. So now, with just a handful of dollars in my pocket, it is time to cash in on my hard work.

It's odd to think how someone you knew only for the first six years of your life can affect the core of who you are.

But of course, it makes sense. It's when we are our most open, vulnerable, impressionable. From my grandfather, I learned to have the courage to pivot, face life with optimism, relentlessly believe in myself, and always forge my own path.

My grandfather, E.B. Boston, was one of those people who was bigger than life. He filled the room with his low laugh, his stories, often with a sweet cloud of pipe smoke encasing him. You could tell he was in a room before you got there, knew he had recently been there because of that familiar scent. I still have an old shirt of his upstairs in the attic in a black zippered bag. When I open that bag, over forty-five years later, and hold it to my face, *I can smell him still.* An embroidered cattleman's long-sleeved button-down, black with white ribbing, cream scalloped shoulder detail with pink roses and green stems weaving down the front, interrupted by mother-of-pearl magnetic buttons. I sometimes enjoy lifting those buttons on and off, listening to the little snap of the magnets, feeling the satisfying pull as they reconnect.

He was over six feet tall, with a strong, square-shouldered build. Athletic and smooth moving, impressive for a person who had his leg nearly severed when he was a child. Sparkling hazel eyes lined with smile wrinkles, a decent amount of speckled-gray, wavy hair, and a sense of style brimming with confidence. Often with plaid pants or a plaid suit jacket, sometimes with both in conflicting patterns. Walking down the street of our wealthy suburb of Chicago, a jolt of energy would rush through me every time someone stared, sniggered, or whispered to a friend. We *owned* that sidewalk, our brashness bolstered by the confusion of others. E.B. was a shining beacon, a great listener, a host and friend to all.

He walked, strongly but stiffly, always supporting himself with one or two canes. As a teenager, while working the farm, E.B. had a devastating accident. He became lodged in a piece of farm equipment, his left leg almost cut off above the knee. It should have been a death sentence. Certainly in isolated rural Appalachia, before reattachment of limbs was a thing attempted. Not to mention sterile operating areas, or even an operating area at all, or antibiotics or antiseptic or pain medication or anything at all. There was absolutely nothing that indicated that he could survive.

But his father was nearby, quickly tied something around his thigh, threw him over the back of a horse, and raced like a madman to find the vet. There was no doctor in Sulphur Well. The homestead was quite a bit outside of "town," which consisted of a small general store and a stinky sulfur pond. When he found the vet at a neighboring farm, he hollered, "*Sew his leg back on!*"

The vet, apparently, and I can just imagine this exchange, said, "We don't even know how to do that. No one knows how to do that."

It was 1915.

My great-grandfather then took out his gun, held it to the vet's head, and said, slowly and clearly, "*Sew his leg back on.*"

And so he did. Somehow. My great-grandfather still holding the gun, the vet did everything he could to save the boy's life while fearing for his own.

And, again somehow, as E.B. used to tell me while he was rubbing the feeling back into his leg, they attached enough of the right tubes to make it possible for him to eventually get back up out of bed and start his life again. It was funny, the way he described it, always a little differently, and it was odd how he walked with his legs at a ninety-degree angle from one another, the left one pointing out while the right pointed forward.

Sulphur Well, back in the day, had one school, which went until eighth grade. Most people didn't make it nearly that far, but E.B. did, finishing just before that fateful day. And when he regained enough strength, he decided to do something that no one in his family had ever done. Change direction. Leave Sulphur Well to continue his education. He could have stayed, I guess, but it was clear that every person living on that destitute homestead needed to be working. There was no extra of anything, and he knew it was go and live or stay and die.

One of the biggest lessons I learn from my grandfather is the bravery to start new. When someone or something tells you no, just go a different direction. Don't wait around and argue about it. Don't try to change anyone's opinion. Don't slow down. Just go about your life in another way. That's what he did by leaving Sulphur Well. He just went a different way. And he did so with flair.

When I am gearing up to leave home, I think back to E.B. and what that must have felt like for him, and it gives me the courage to follow in his footsteps. He often talked to me about his decisions, his need to push forward in his own life. We'd sit around playing cards, the smell of popping popcorn coming from the fireplace. He'd tell me there was a state boarding high school in a town about forty-five minutes away from Sulphur Well. He applied, was admitted to the school, stubbornly regained his health, made his way there, and believed in himself enough to take that one-way journey.

It takes confidence, but also patience, planning, and cunning to set up a new life for yourself. You have to be organized. Finances, travel, housing, and entry into an existing structure all have to be dealt with. I have been planning my transition away from home for an entire year. I apply to the program in Minnesota, sending transcripts as well as recordings of my violin playing to the music school. I work and save every penny, babysitting and playing my violin for weddings. I have to figure out how to buy a plane ticket, travel as an unaccompanied minor, and decide what of my belongings will fit into a backpack. And when I arrive, I have to hit the ground running. I need to be a success as a college student, find a job in three weeks, and keep on practicing. I don't plan on being at the University of Minnesota for too long. I have bigger plans, and I am going to have to work my butt off to make them happen. My heart is set on going to the Curtis Institute of Music in two years—arguably the best music school in the world, it's the hardest school to get into in North America, and it is tuition free.

In my personal slide show of cherished memories is a freeze-frame of E.B. and me at opposite ends of a dark red, nubby ottoman in our living room, staring down in hushed concentration. A deck of cards is laid out in a grid, the corner ones precariously holding on as the footstool curves downwards. We play yet another round of memory. Word on the street is that he can memorize three decks at a time and is an unbeatable poker player. But more than that, he is just a great guy to be around. You feel a glow. A happiness. It takes me years to realize that he is unusual in this way. There is always a hearty hello, a back slap, a handshake. Or a more formal greeting, followed by asking about specific members of the family, remembering details about illnesses, births, accomplishments or struggles. Stories, hilarious anecdotes, drawing people around him to share his unique experiences and philosophy of life.

I remember traveling through a room at the big fancy parties my mother threw in the house in Glenview, Illinois. Chandeliers sparkling, fur coats jockeying for space in the front closets, hired servers with finger foods, a manned bar, me with a silver bell on a cushion to announce dinner. And there is E.B., born and raised in just about the most desperate surroundings I have ever seen, listening and chatting with the jewel-encrusted ladies, then turning around to do card tricks for the kids. He teaches me how to burp, and I spend many an hour cultivating and expanding my repertoire. As I circle the rooms, inviting people to the dining room for dinner, with my velvet dress and patent leather Mary Janes, I also ask people if they would like to hear my collection of burps. A yes sets off about a minute of various length and textured belches, some long enough for me to burp the alphabet. I have begun to understand that you can be ridiculous and silly and formal, surprising and charming, all at the same time.

𝄐

When I leave home, I am ready to work hard. My parents don't think I will make it, telling me I will not find a way of supporting myself. They're not going to fund me in this "rash" decision. I am going to be on my own from here on out. Maybe they are trying to scare me, but it makes me even more determined. I figure I have to make $600 a month to pay rent and cover food and various sundry. I send my resume to all of the small orchestras in the Twin Cities to see if I can get work, and when I arrive, I find a store to sell my homemade jewelry. But I need steady money, *now*. I have a three-week deadline. I can't impose on my sister any longer than that. She is trying to make it herself and can't support another person.

Looking through the "help wanted" section in the paper, I find what I am looking for: "experienced strolling violinist needed for buffet night at Donatelli's Italian Restaurant, pay $75 for three hours per week." *This I can do.* I memorize twenty songs (Italian street songs, light classics, and opera arias). I show up dressed in borrowed casual evening wear, telling the proprietress I am twenty years old and have years of experience strolling in Chicago. They hire me on the spot. For half the amount I need to survive. I say I would be delighted to start next week with $50 an hour, not the $25 advertised, and they know how to contact me. I turn and walk away, doing my best to look confident, shaking inside, wondering if they will take the bait. This is my last chance at making it; I'm down to my last $20. If I find a retail job, I'll have to put in too many hours to make rent, and I need all the time I can get to practice. I plan on putting in five hours of personal practice a day, the minimum I need in order to prepare for my next goal.

Donatelli's calls the next day, and I happily stroll for them every Wednesday for the next two years. It becomes a home away from home as I get to know the staff, regulars, and family, always returning to our apartment with a bag of delicious, rustic Italian leftovers from the buffet table. I learn how to work a room, what kinds of music suit different groups of people, how to make small talk with all kinds of customers. It is very different from playing the Bruch *Violin Concerto* with an orchestra at a concert. My audience is right there, and I find how to play for them in a way that makes them immediately happy, has them singing along. And the tips show that it's working. Within a couple of months, I have enough memorized material that I can go the entire three hours without checking my music or set sheet. Donatelli's is one of my most cherished memories of my time in the Twin Cities. It's not long before my sister and I move into a bigger apartment, where I have my own room, and my ulcer begins its slow healing.

E.B. graduates from college and moves to Chicago, and I think his talent at cards and ability to get along with anyone lands him right where he can flourish. Gangsters, prohibition, fast living, and a place for dreamers, gamblers, and movers and shakers. The devastatingly wealthy and those who pull themselves up by their bootstraps rub shoulders. It's about smarts, being fearless, and carving your own path.

He has a job as an engineer, but on his own time he begins to invent things and sell the patents. He starts his own company, designing and installing heating systems for the huge new buildings going up in the booming expansion of Chicago. The Art Deco craze, the sumptuous and daring explosion of skyscrapers. These buildings need heating, and E.B. positions himself to supply it for them. I remember going to his warehouse. It seems impossibly large, an entire city block, with a rough section for offices raised above the floor on stilts, with neatly organized, gigantic heating duct supplies as far as the eye can see. He begins to regularly send money back to Sulphur Well and starts to move into high society.

E.B. loves telling me stories about his past, usually with a large tumbler in his hand filled with a dark, translucent drink. His tales are accompanied by the clink of ice cubes, the puff of a pipe. One of his favorite topics is the 1933 Century of Progress World's Fair, an exposition celebrating the centennial of Chicago. It was a huge, yearlong science and industry fair. The motto, "Science

Finds, Industry Applies, Man Conforms," is everything Chicago stands for and is right up E.B.'s alley. He tells me how he and a couple of his buddies rented a stall and sold two things. One was an early prototype Band-Aid, which E.B. describes as a piece of gauze stuck on some adhesive tape. The second was "Relics of the True Cross." I mean, who *wouldn't* want a bonafide piece of the cross Jesus was crucified on?

They made both of these things down in the basement, dyeing splinters of wood and cutting gauze and tape. He laughs as he explains how the "Relics of the True Cross" sold like hotcakes, but no one liked the bandages. He invents other stuff, or at least imagines it. A man-made imitation wood, similar to Formica. Metal straws in all colors. And the underwater bicycle, for example. I still wear his silver ring from the Century of Progress World's Fair. Rectangular, adjustable, with the words "I Will" on the bottom. E.B. makes enough money during that time to afford a *very* comfortable life.

There was a lot going on in my life then that wasn't about me and E.B. My violin life, my family. But in my memories, thick with his Kentucky drawl, his faraway look as he reaches slowly for his tobacco pouch, packing in fresh leaf, lighting a match, and puff puff puff, puffffff, it's just the two of us.

I am not always sure if the things I remember about him were told to me by him, by my mother, during my visits to Kentucky, or just plain made up in my own head, and it doesn't matter. What I remember is every bit as real as holding one of his old poker chips to my cheek, surprisingly smooth and cold. It is inside of me. The belief in a life fully lived, in a life worth fighting for. He had left a trust for me to use to buy a violin when I turned fourteen years old. And every day, for hours upon hours, I hold my violin under my chin, coaxing stories and memories from that living piece of wood. That glorious violin that he gave to me ensures I will have him with me forever. Through that instrument, he has traveled the world with me as I give voice to my deepest thoughts and dreams.

He died when I was six, on a snowy Christmas Day, right after my family had made our big move to Winnetka, Illinois. To the house that would, a mere ten years later, become the iconic house in the movie *Home Alone*.

3
Burned Out

Life doesn't go in a smooth line, or follow the same tempo from beginning to end, like a perpetual motion. It's more like a mosaic; a pretty piece of stone here and there, some imperfections between sections, and when you step back, you are surprised to see the picture that emerges. The picture you thought you were carefully piecing together doesn't resemble what everyone else sees as the story of *your* life. Those endless days when you fall in love for the first time, or how all of seventh grade seems like it takes one minute. Holding your grandfather's hand as he passes away was years ago. A single moment can change the entire trajectory of your life.

The story that was written for me by my parents doesn't end up being my story at all. Or maybe it does, in some convoluted way, but the journey towards that destination is more like a scavenger hunt and less like the carefully curated path my mother had planned for me.

When I was eighteen, after years of training, competition, travel, performance, and intense one-on-one work with master violinists, I was accepted into the Curtis Institute of Music, an elite music conservatory housed in a series of inter-connected mansions in downtown Philadelphia. It's the most selective college in North America, with a lower acceptance rate than Stanford or Harvard University, and caters to the cream of the crop of highly trained musicians.

Sitting on a curved metal bench under the leafy trees of Rittenhouse Square, one hears music wafting from the stately white mansions. Singers, pianists, violinists—you can listen to the stars of tomorrow for free any day of the week, if you pick your bench correctly. Inside these buildings, the wood-paneled walls, velvet-covered furniture, original oil paintings, and Wednesday high teas give every moment a feeling of luxury and privilege. Hard-earned privilege, as each person who belongs to Curtis has spent their entire life working towards artistic achievement and is, indeed, a legend in the making. Lang Lang, Leonard Bernstein, Hilary Hahn, Yuja Wang, and Samuel Barber are alumni, and Curtis graduates make up a third of the membership of the top-five orchestras in the United States: Boston, Chicago, Cleveland, New York, and Philadelphia. In fact, half of the Philadelphia Orchestra are Curtis graduates.

It's like attending a school of gold-medal Olympic athletes, where every student has headshots, management, professional international engagements, and recording contracts. While I do have a certain amount of name recognition, a tidy list of competition wins, and publicity photos, I certainly don't have management or a full concert calendar. It is shocking to flip through music magazines in the library and regularly recognize students in my class. While I am there, over half of the student body (155 full-scholarship students) is from overseas, many having been personally selected or recruited by members of the faculty. There is a 3:2 student-faculty ratio, and the faculty themselves are world-renowned superstars with full schedules. You can also take classes for free at

the University of Pennsylvania, no application required. Curtis itself doesn't require SAT scores. It is understood that if you are good enough to be accepted, the skills that you have, to be as advanced as you are on your instrument, mean that you will excel in any program.

My class schedule comprises the regular coursework of a degree in music, including a variety of performance-based classes. Weekly private lessons, chamber music coachings, piano lessons, twice-weekly orchestra, solo performances, theory, ear training, solfège, music history, as well as the classes I need to fulfill a bachelor's degree. Many Curtis grads will have international careers, so language acquisitions are stressed, and most students pursue several. There are more than twenty nations represented in the student body I'm part of, and it seems to me that most members of the Curtis family, from students to teachers to administrators, are already bi- or trilingual.

Hilary Hahn (who today commands one of the most impressive appearance fees in the classical music world) is in my German class, and, as an eleven-year-old, lives in a high-rise with her pet guinea pig, Penelope, making her own meals, being tutored, practicing, and performing. Her parents still live mostly in Baltimore, where she grew up, and come up to stay with her, but from my perspective, she seems to be on her own.

She asks me over for lunch after class, and we walk across Locust Street and enter a tall building, taking the elevator up to an apartment looking over Rittenhouse Square. It's modest, sparse, and impeccably clean. Her kitchen opens to the living room and has a large cage on the counter. She introduces me to her adorable piggy, giving her a bit of something green from the fridge as she happily squeaks her greeting.

I am surprised to see no evidence of a parent in the space, only a couple of pairs of child-sized shoes lined up by the front door, and a little coat hanging on a hook. She makes tuna sandwiches and strawberry smoothies for us, and I think to myself, *Here is a child, making a well-rounded and healthy lunch for me.* I am seven years her senior, and my apartment isn't nearly as well put together as this. She is poised and quiet, and as she pulls the Tupperware out of the fridge, she explains her recipe: the secret ingredient is pickles, she exclaims! She starts the blender, and I spend some quality time with Penelope. Soft, warm, eager to engage. I can tell that this creature gets a lot of attention; she isn't afraid, or hiding in her house like many guinea pigs do. She is a cute, social fuzzball, and I am suddenly sad. A little girl alone in a big world, with only a guinea pig to come home to. If you look up Hilary today, you can find videos of her with her current guinea pigs; clips of her practicing next to the cage, stopping to talk to them or give them a treat.

Our conversation is hesitant, until she asks me about my practice schedule, how I organize my time.

"Basically, I do five hours a day, starting with two of scales and etudes. An hour of Bach, then two of my concerto. I add on time for extra things like a show piece or orchestra stuff, chamber music."

"Oh, that's pretty organized. Sounds good!" she says.

"Yeah, I of course divide the pieces into sections, assigned to days of the week, and go for large play-throughs on the weekends to get ready for my lesson." I say, feeling pretty secure in my tried-and-true method.

"How about you—what's your schedule look like?" I ask.

I am floored with the detail and impressive construction of her practice method. She structurally analyzes her pieces, working on parallel sections to highlight contrasts and similarities, and the amount and level of repertoire dwarfs my own schedule. She also moves much more quickly through pieces, getting to the final, concert-ready stage many times faster than I could possibly do. She is super sweet and nice, but for some reason, instead of inspired, I feel dejected and unworthy. *I am so far behind that I will never catch up.* I am hopeless.

One day after class, in my last year at Curtis, she asks me if I would like to go to hear a concert she is playing. It's a matinee; her mother isn't in town and she would love some company. I am very happy to be asked, and the next afternoon as we walk together the couple of blocks to the Academy of Music, a gorgeous concert hall built in the mid-1800s, it slowly becomes clear that this is no ordinary performance: Hilary is the *soloist* with the Philadelphia Orchestra, one of the best orchestras in the world. It is her debut performance with the orchestra, I later find out. She is wearing a puffy velvet and satin knee-length dress, and as we enter the backstage area, she asks if I can just stand there with her before she goes out and if I can watch from the wings so she will know I am there.

She is stunning. *So confident.* With a shockingly rich, deep tone and a unique sentiment, her command of the instrument and mesmerizing interpretation pulls the audience in, hanging on every note. The turn of a phrase, a slide put precisely here or there, shows that she has a deep knowledge of the past masters of the instrument. She stands still, with a personal approach, not pandering to the audience as many young players are encouraged to do. Her tone production is massive, and her technique flawless.

As the audience thunders their applause, it seems clear to me, and everyone in that hall, that we are witnessing the dawning of one of the most remarkable artists of this century. The orchestra themselves begin to pound their feet and tap their bows on the stands, creating a special cacophony which rarely emanates from the opinionated and sometimes bitter ranks of top orchestras. She has it, and we all can tell. Smiling as she comes back after her bows, she thanks me quietly for coming to be with her that day. It's only now, when I see my own young daughters, that I can fully appreciate her bravery, her work ethic, and her quiet confidence, all of which was rigorously hard-earned.

At Curtis, I am a full-scholarship student, but there is still rent, food, and sundries to cover. My mother sends me small checks, but they don't make a significant dent in my needs. I have to find ways of making money while still putting in the necessary hours of practice and study. My jobs during those years in Philadelphia run the gamut of playing as a substitute in orchestras, shelving for the Curtis library, data entry for the alumni office, hostessing at a restaurant, making and selling jewelry and clothing I design, and reading the *Wall Street Journal* for an hour every morning to an elderly, blind dowager.

She lives in the penthouse of a building close to school, and as the doorman calls up, at 6 am every day, I am ushered into the elevator, where a special key is inserted to access the top floors. The elevator opens directly into her apartment, and as the maid (yes, with the little white cap and white apron) welcomes me, two snow-white, miniature daemons perform impossible bouncing maneuvers on their spindly back legs, yapping and baring their teeth. I am shown into the drawing room, followed by these nasty little puffballs, where my hostess is comfortably settled into a damask-covered love seat, in a crisp outfit, hair coifed, and with a tray to her side on which tea and a plate of perfectly formed nibbles are laid. My seat, a Queen Anne covered in crushed velvet, is directly opposite her, and *my* table has a tall glass of ice water on a coaster and the day's *Wall Street Journal.*

We start with pleasantries: the weather, how school is going, etc.

"Good morning, dear, how was your lesson this week with Mr. Galimir?" she asks.

"Good, thank you. We are working on the Ravel *Sonata* this week."

"I understand Mr. Galimir worked with Maurice Ravel directly."

"Yes, he speaks fondly of those times. In fact, he made the first recording of the Ravel *Quartet* as a young man in Vienna, playing in his family quartet with his sisters, in the '30s, between the wars."

I read the headlines on page one. She asks me to repeat things, more clearly. I do my best to enunciate, pretending I am minor royalty visiting the queen. She asks my opinion on the news. Mild conversation, never dipping into the unseemly or provocative, ensues. The maid checks in every fifteen minutes to refresh beverages, and by the end of the hour, I am up to date on current world affairs, my voice hoarse and throat sore. She is nice enough, the dowager, and this job gives me plenty of preparation for later on in life when I will need to speak at length to patrons and concertgoers after performances or at receptions. Talk about absolutely nothing, avoid all controversy, and skirt politics. Find some way to agree with the person, stay calm, and be adept at changing topics without the other person noticing. *Good stuff.* The maid hands me an envelope with a twenty-dollar bill inside as I step into the wallpapered elevator, heading back to school.

My life at Curtis slowly begins to weigh heavily on me. I am no Hilary. No Yuja or Lang Lang. *What am I even doing here?* I am swimming in feelings of inadequacy, however imagined or real. When I'm not at school, not in Philadelphia, I take the stage confidently. I am a star performer still. But I don't have the inner strength, the talent or technique to rise to the top, or even float in the middle, of this extraordinary school. I begin to sink, and my teacher isn't able to or interested in saving me. There are plenty of stars to foster, and so the chaff is left to fend for itself.

But I make it through. I take my degree and walk away, disillusioned. I walk away from that world, away from classical music, and away from everything I have built in what seems to have already been a very long life. *I am twenty and done.*

In my apartment on Spruce Street in downtown Philadelphia, I give myself some time to plot my next step. I get a call from the Juilliard School in New York City offering me a full scholarship starting the next year, no audition necessary. I know I should accept, but I am too close to it all. Insecure. *I just don't get it anymore.* What does classical music have to do with real life, with current events or regular people? Why spend these never-ending hours perfecting minutiae that only the smallest percentage of the population can even understand or hear? And do I even like the people who can hear if my octave runs in a Paganini *Caprice* (the most difficult music written for violin; each of the twenty-four short, unaccompanied pieces can take hundreds of hours to be performance ready) are perfectly in tune, with clear bow technique and a musical vision? It is exactly those people

I am sick of. Petty, competitive, stuck-up, boring rule-followers. It's not their fault, exactly. It's the nature of the game, to fight your way to the top and then do anything you can to remain king of the hill, no matter who you have to push aside to stay there.

I am also reeling from the end of a three-year relationship that was weeks away from the altar. *Dress*, check, *venue*, check, *bridal shower*, check, *insane fiancé*, check. Stephen swept me off my feet. A commanding presence, with black, wavy hair; great at languages. Gorgeous. Misty eyes and luxurious lashes, he has a chiseled jaw that pulses when he is studying. Stephen is as brilliant as he is complicated. He is so serious, mature—he's a few years older than me and has a carefully constructed air of old-school money, with his crisp shirts, loafers. We had dated intensely as students in college—he left his fiancée to be with me—and he follows me to Philadelphia, arriving partway through my first year, getting a job and moving in with me. I know it's a bad idea for me to be distracted from my studies, but we are swimming in the mania and delusion of obsessive love.

I can't tell if it's me or him who starts to go crazy. It starts so slowly, I don't know if I am imagining things or not. He adores me, wants to be with me every second of the day, lavishes me with affection. He waits for me by the entrance to school after class, to walk me home. He tells me he loves my hair down, how great I look in that red skirt. Soon he is telling me that if I wear my hair up in a bun, I act differently; just keep it down. When I come out of the bedroom in jeans, he tells me to go change, picking out a different outfit for me. Soon, everything I wear, everyone I hang out with, has to be approved by him. He suggests who I should try to befriend. Before I even realize it, I am isolated. Eventually he even tries to convince me that I have a dual personality. On his urging, I begin to see a therapist, who listens intently but *clearly* doesn't share his opinion.

Sitting alone on the floor of my apartment, I suddenly wake up about Stephen. It seems to me that he had managed to control everything I was doing, everything I wore, what I said to other people. I have lost myself, lost my way. I gather myself, and with determination, I give him the boot. He was, despite all the messed-up stuff and the damage I sustained, a great and deep love of mine.

Years later, I find out that Stephen is living in a mental institution in a small, rural town, close to his mother, and as far as I know, lives there still. I went to visit him a number of years ago with a friend, and as he talked to me, he kept one eye closed, squinching up that side of his face. With his mellifluous voice, he calmly explained that he keeps that side of his face closed so people do not see his other personality.

I also wake up about classical music. I need a break. From love, from responsibility, from the career track that I have been on since before I can remember. I say no to Juilliard, no to Stephen, and buy an old clunker Buick Skylark, throw in my violin and a couple of suitcases, and head west. All the way west, to Portland, Oregon. My old high school friend Lucy has contacted me. She's dropped out of Reed College, is pregnant, living on a commune, and wants me to come to her home birth. It is just the call I have been waiting for. *Hello, World, here I come!*

The commune is in a rundown neighborhood of Portland, in a big gray Craftsman house with a large porch and a decent but dusty backyard. I ring the doorbell and Lucy comes out, looking both the same as ever and different. Her large belly is pushing at the fabric of her tie-dyed dress, and her once long blond hair, now cropped close to her scalp, looks like she shaved it herself, all uneven and pokey. She has always been a vibrant, creative person, but now I can see her in a new light, one that has created responsibility and reliability in her, not attributes that I would have previously thought of when thinking of Lucy.

𝄐

Lucy and I meet when we are both members of the Chicago Youth Symphony, six years before I go to join her in Oregon. Lucy drives in every Saturday morning from a western suburb and I come down from the north. I am leading a section, the soloist in Saint-Saëns' devilishly difficult *Introduction and Rondo Capriccioso* for violin and orchestra, and Lucy is last chair. We share the elevator up to the tenth floor of the Fine Arts Building on Michigan Avenue in downtown Chicago one day, and Lucy is having a silly conversation with the elevator operator (it is one of the only remaining buildings in the city with an original elevator, manually run by a couple of old guys in funny outfits and pillbox hats). They speak to each other like old friends, and as we leave the elevator, I introduce myself to Lucy, who almost instantly becomes a good friend.

I am dying to get away from the intensely competitive clique in the front row of the orchestra, away from people I know from Winnetka and Highland Park, rich suburbs (think *Ferris Bueller's Day Off*, which was filmed in my neighborhood) filled with overachievers. Lucy, who has a sister and a single mom who works 9-5, is from a blue-collar town, lives in an apartment, and seems entirely alien to me. She knows she isn't a standout in orchestra and is happy to just sit in the back. She is quick, sassy, and up for any kind of mischief we can possibly manage in our weekly fifteen minutes of break time together. While I am the soloist in Orchestra Hall that season, she is chilling in the back, cracking jokes with the percussion section and just goofing around. We sneak smokes with the guys in the percussion and bass sections during breaks, hanging off the fire escape or slipping back behind the building by the dumpsters. And Lucy seems to be a *really good kisser*, something I haven't had much chance to delve into, personally. She practices kissing with a variety of guys from the percussion, bass, and brass sections, in a casual kind of way. I am *totally* impressed.

We see each other every Saturday, and when prom season rolls around, Lucy (who is a couple of years older than me) calls and says her boyfriend has a friend and maybe I would like to come along as his date? This is fantastic! The last thing I want to do is go to my own prom, and I'm not old enough yet anyway. Besides, my violin teacher forbids the girls she teaches from dating, saying that by the time you start dating, go through the relationship, then the terrible breakup, you could have learned a whole violin concerto. Waste of time. Plus, boys are a disaster until about their mid-twenties anyway. Truer words were never said.

So, I think, *what a great opportunity!* My chances to experiment with kissing and anything boy-related have been limited: summer camps, All-State Orchestra retreats. I make the most of any moment to learn a new move or get to the next base. This prom will be a great situation to expand my repertoire with no commitment. *Perfect.*

I design and make my own dress. During those years I mainly wore my own creations, which were quite experimental, made out of old leftover furniture fabric or my own clothes cut up and repurposed: shirts made into skirts and jeans cut up and re-sewn in strips. I also wore mismatched shoes, first starting with different-colored Converse and eventually, at my most confident, one thigh-high boot and one slipper. My prom dress is a contemporary, asymmetrical spin on a flapper dress, which I pair with fishnet stockings and some Adidas.

I can't remember my date's name, but it starts with a Br. Brent is the son of a dentist, wears thick glasses, and is balding prematurely. He is quiet and polite; a perfect person to put in my training program, if only for one night. I am determined to get to the next base, refine some of the things I have tried before, all without skidding into home. And, will wonders never cease, Brady is game. *Very game.* We stay up all night. The next day we head to the Six Flags Great America amusement park where the four of us groggily wander around, avoiding the big rides. We aren't the only post-prom, green-faced, hungover kids listlessly meandering around in crumpled tuxes and evening wear with sweatshirts pulled over top, throwing up in garbage cans. It is a *marvelous* prom, successful in every way.

I guess I hadn't made myself clear, because the next Sunday, Brandon shows up at my house wanting to take me to lunch. He's driven ninety minutes to get there. I explain that I'm not allowed to date because my violin teacher doesn't let us, and that I had a lovely evening with him and wish him a happy life. He walks away looking crestfallen, and as I wave goodbye, I feel just the slightest tug of emotion. He's actually a sweet guy. I quickly go to practice and spend the rest of the day working on my concerto, thanking my lucky stars that my teacher has spared me whatever it is that I've just missed.

Six years on, I drive from Philadelphia to Portland in my new, old Buick. I am so looking forward to connecting again with Lucy after these years apart. *What's her life like now?* What's *my* life like? We had fallen out of touch, but she somehow tracked me down in Philadelphia, called the switchboard at Curtis, and left a note for me with her number. Her invitation comes at a time when I feel so utterly alone, and the idea of living in a close community of people who have no knowledge of me or of music lifts a great weight from my chest.

The commune is made up of a variety of people. In the basement lives a polyamorous family with two females, a male, and six kids. On the first floor are a young couple who work at the food co-op and a single guy in his mid-thirties who works for a nonprofit of some kind. The second and third floors have seven living spaces, filled with small families, single people, and couples. There are people of all ethnic backgrounds, religious people and atheists, ranging in age from one year to sixty-five. The kids are "homeschooled," or, I guess, "un-schooled," because I never see any actual schooling or books or any adults engaging with them in an organized manner. They are a nice, fun pack of feral children, and everyone pitches in and helps them with things like figuring out food or finding some lost object. I'm not sure how many of them there are altogether, and I am not sure anyone really knows. They take care of themselves, mostly. No bedtime, no alarm clocks, mealtimes if they are around, otherwise they concoct stuff in the kitchen that smells surprisingly tasty.

It would be nice if someone, every once in a while, would suggest they bathe in some capacity. The dirt is actually visible, and I swear I can almost see wavy ripples of smell emanating from them, à la the character Pigpen. I even see them occasionally picking chunks of matted stuff off one another casually, like a group of gorillas. Their hair is accidentally dreadlocked in irregular chunks, and I can't really tell one of them from the other, except some are shorter and some taller. At one point, a bathing intervention is instigated by the mother (I think) of a twelve-ish-year-old child. After quite a bit of running around the house and loud complaining, they get in the bath and let their mom soak and scrub them. Their hair is beyond help, and the person who emerges from that bathroom is someone I have never met before. An entirely different color, with short hair and fresh clothes that are new to me. Unfortunately, none of the other members of the wild pack think the bath looked like a particularly good idea, so that little person just sticks out like a clean thumb for the next couple of weeks, smearing dirt and mud on themself in attempts to fit in again with their peers.

Lucy has the front-facing room on the top floor, with sharply angled ceilings. I have to crouch most of the time, and I sleep on a camping pad on the floor next to her single mattress. There are three bathrooms in the house, two with showers. Each person is assigned a particular bathroom, and next to the toilet there is a row of hooks. Your name is written above your hook on a piece of masking tape, and from the hook hangs your personal cloth for wiping your natural, organic bum. There is no toilet paper, and flushing is done with a pitcher of collected rainwater from large barrels which have been replenished during the rainy season.

My days are filled with helping with food preparation, hunting for mushrooms in the forest to sell to the co-op, and accompanying Lucy to her doula and midwife appointments. It is a vegan, no-wheat, and no-sugar house, and the single guy from the first floor is a fruitarian. He is the skinniest person I have ever met and is kind of translucent. Behind his back, I refer to him as the *Translucent Bird*. We have communal meals, with a chart for prep, cooking, and cleanup.

Evenings at the commune are pretty wacky, with members of the house and random other people hanging out on the porch or in the living room, smoking weed and consuming mushrooms and I don't even know what else. I am still shell-shocked from my breakup with Stephen, and this place shows me that relationships don't need to be long, serious, well-matched, or between particular genders, if you even believe in something as dated as genders. By observation and integration, I begin to feel released from my years under Stephen, finding a flow and freedom to everything I do or don't do. At night, there is always someone playing mbira or guitar and singing, and on Saturdays, I go play my violin downtown by the farmer's market to save up cash for the next adventure in my life.

The commune has an interesting financial structure. At the end of every month, the amount of rent and expenses is estimated for the next month. Then, every member writes down what they can contribute, folds the paper, and puts it in a drawstring satchel. One person (rotating each month) tallies the amount and lets us know if we are short, necessitating another round, keeping the information in the hat to themselves. They believe that no one should know how much the others pay and that monthly incomes and responsibilities naturally fluctuate.

Lucy works for a nonprofit rehab clinic for pimps

who have been released from prison, giving them work training in the hope that they will not bounce back to their former professions as business managers for prostitutes. It is a cool way to look at the situation, one that historically pigeonholes the prostitutes, sending them to prison or vilifying them. This takes a look at their actual, *I don't know*, captors and tries to find a way out of the endless cycle by digging in a different direction. It is satisfying work for her, and I attend several meetings and protests for various social issues during my time here. This female-centered view opens my eyes to the world, and I realize that I, a classical musician who has played my whole life, have never actually learned a piece by a female composer or been conducted in an orchestra by a woman. It is a first step towards a new view for me, an eye-opening moment in my life.

Lucy has the quintessential doula/midwife home birth, complete with all of the accoutrements. There is a drum circle, bodily fluids of all stripe, moaning, bravery, and, of course, the eating of the placenta. Cooked with garlic, oregano, and olive oil, *thank you very much*.

I stay for another month here, in this free, unique place, where no one wonders what I do for a "living" or asks me to do anything I don't want to do. Before leaving, I pick up a bunch of half-used buckets of paint from the recycled home repair store, and as a group, we paint my Buick Skylark for the trip back east. A large rainbow octopus on the roof sends her tentacles down the car, adorned with children's handprints and flowers. And I am finally free—free of the expectations that I had allowed others to place on me and that I had indeed placed on myself. I decide to head to Oberlin, Ohio, where my childhood teachers, a husband-and-wife team, offer to give me some violin lessons and a place to stay in return for housecleaning, while I figure out my next step. I'm not sure what I want to do, but I think maybe a degree in Women's Studies could be interesting. I forgive myself for not deciding to go to Juilliard, and I am over Stephen.

As I turn over the ignition, I pop a Cat Stevens tape into the cassette player, reaching for a crumpled pack of Marlboro Reds. I am ready.

※ 4
Cake

The gynecologist has her ultrasound wand on my stomach, the light blue, cold, jiggly jelly squishing onto my exposed belly, and she says it just like she is ordering a coffee:

"Only one heartbeat today. Single fetal demise. Most likely it will be absorbed by the living fetus, but we'll keep our eyes out for complications. You might have some cramping and bleeding, but that's absolutely normal, and of course the other fetus is now high-risk. Would you like a copy of your ultrasound today?"

It feels like someone just dropped a concrete brick on my head; air is escaping my lungs and it's difficult to breathe in. I look up at Jason, his eyes closed, standing so still. This is not the first loss we have had; this is the one that has stuck it out the longest, the one that gives me tiny shivers of hope, the one that makes me look at the study on the second floor of our house and imagine a crib instead of a desk. Not yet, though. Still a long way to go before that furniture swap is made.

I sink into the reclined, faux-leather examining bed, the cold stirrups and the flimsy draped paper rectangle covering my knees. The leather's as fake as the doctor's bedside manner. She doesn't even blink, offer consolation or a kind look. She must have seen this hundreds of times, I suppose. But after all these years, the adoption process we'd embarked on, the doctors and fertility treatments, I could use a soft hand on my shoulder. A hesitation, an apologetic sadness in her voice. I will never return to this office. The pain of this cold encounter stings with its efficiency, officiousness. I decide to research and find a practice with midwives and a doula instead.

The next office is warm, almost Oregonian in its wooden-plank house down a long winding road, with midwives and gynecologists working together in a practice, support groups in the evenings, lactation consultants for after. I am thirty-seven, living in Middletown, Connecticut, and tentatively *so very happy* that we have one healthy possibility in the oven. (One who right now has her driver's permit, dyed-purple hair, and is often found in the living room on a blue couch, playing a pink ukulele and singing Beatles tunes.)

The pregnancy is not easy. Severe exhaustion, morning sickness that lasts all day, all through the pregnancy, and lower back pain that regularly sends electric shocks all the way to my toes. My body doesn't like to hold on to fetuses; my uterus is inhospitable, they tell me. I had already moved on years ago from my regular doctor. Her advice was to make sure I tried to get pregnant when I was ovulating—*not very helpful.* I go to several different gynecologists and eventually to a fabulous fertility clinic. After testing, they say my eggs are good, Jason's sperm is excellent, and I have a problem with my uterine lining. The suggestion for IUI (also known as artificial insemination) is something I can agree to. Forcing my body to release more eggs, weeding out Jason's semen to have only the best possible swimmers, and giving the embryo a welcoming, happy uterus is the way to go. I have to keep my uterus healthy with hormonal supplements, and I continue my weekly appointments with a reproductive acupuncturist in New Haven, surrounded by pastel-colored walls, light incense, and soothing waterfall sounds. I don't know if these appointments are a bunch of bunkum, but I am ready and eager to try anything, and that hour every week is a welcome change from my normal schedule of teaching, rehearsing, and touring.

It has been a long time getting here, to this fragile pregnancy. As a woman in a classical performance career, it is exceedingly difficult to start a family. If you are in a full-time orchestra, it is possible to have a relatively normal life. Stable schedule, solid finances, and health benefits. You can even possibly meet someone you might want to have a long-term relationship with! But a chamber music career, that's very difficult. When you're on the road more than half of the year, it's almost impossible to find or retain a partner who will tolerate your many irregular absences, your late nights and early mornings, your incessant practice and rehearsal. When you return home after tour, the note on the kitchen counter says they need a break from this relationship, they need something steady and normal. It's an amazing and fulfilling career, but the toll on your personal life is significant. As a chamber musician, most of your concerts are booked two years in advance, which means if you do manage to get pregnant, your manager will have to cancel concerts, find a replacement, or re-book, putting a huge strain on your colleagues, presenters, and managers.

If you are a female soloist? Basically forget it. There are exceptions, but only at the very tippy top of the career ladder, where the soloist has some say in her schedule. For the rest of the female soloists, there are the years where you are fighting your way to the top with competitions, building a career, traveling constantly, and taking the time and considerable effort to look absolutely fabulous while doing it. By the time you realize you might want to have a baby, it's too late, you can't manage to hold on to a partner, and your manager might fire you. You can't take time off because there are a hundred hungry violinists waiting to take your spot, biding their time for your moment of weakness. All that work for nothing. There you are, forty-five years old, giving yourself daily injections, paying tens of thousands of dollars for your third round of IVF, and going to play the Brahms *Violin Concerto* in Helsinki the next day. *You get the picture.*

When I begin trying to have a baby, I have a pretty sweet life: interesting and varied education, a teaching position at a music school that I stepped into right after graduating with my master's in music performance. I've bought a charming farmhouse in Connecticut close enough to zip into New York City in less than two hours; I play with inspiring musicians, and my trio has a forty-concert-a-year touring schedule; and Jason is not only a terrific partner, he is in my trio. *Ideal.* Perfect, in fact. But when I hit my early thirties, I want it all. And I'm not going to take no for an answer.

Our manager books us high-level concerts with good fees and organizes tours with efficiency. Not like other managers I have been with, who schedule one concert in Wichita, then one in Seattle, then off to New Orleans, creating nightmare travel situations. Our manager has a good office, friendly staff, and the other groups and soloists on the roster are spectacular. When we sit down for our yearly meeting, I realize I am going to have to be even more determined to have a baby than I had anticipated. Jason and I are in the midst of searching for a new pianist for our trio, and the first thing our manager says is that if we choose a woman, we will have to find another agent. Women my age are unreliable. They start families and make life hell for managers. There are plenty of good male pianists around, so his advice is to choose one of them.

And, also, if I am starting to think about getting pregnant, make damn sure I plan it so I give birth in December. That's the slow period for bookings, and he doesn't fancy making more work for himself if I decide to give birth in peak season like October or March. I am supposed to be organized and thoughtful with my life so as not to inconvenience him. He makes this clear.

And so, for several years, we try to honor his wishes. The problem is that April, our target month to get pregnant, is an unusually busy time. At the university, it's recital season, with extra lessons and a lot of late nights. Add on to that the regular touring schedule and the window of opportunity is narrow, to say the least. And this is before I even know I am the owner of an inhospitable uterus. After a couple of years of this, and of course choosing an amazing male pianist, nothing is working. A friend of mine, who is a member of a high-powered string quartet and has a young child, sits me down and tells me to stop dithering around and commit to starting a family. She is with the same manager and has been given the same spiel (which he only gives in person, not wanting to leave a paper trail), and she says to me that time is ticking, it is very difficult to get pregnant at all with a touring career, and I need to buckle down and get serious with my plans.

It's the wake-up call I need.

For another year, we attempt to start a family. After numerous setbacks and early disappointments, it becomes clear that we need to explore alternative options. We reach out to several adoption agencies but immediately face rejections for two primary reasons. First, we are not married, just domestic partners. We are happy to get married right now, but it won't help. The requirement is that you need to have been married for at least three years, which will delay our process even further. Second, we are not Christian. Many adoption agencies are affiliated with Christian organizations, and most of the children they work with come from religious backgrounds. These agencies have the discretion to choose the adoptive parents and prefer not to place children with unmarried couples who do not share their religious beliefs. Two un-hitched atheists from Connecticut aren't going to cut it.

Eventually, we discover an adoption agency in New Haven—a small organization that works with single individuals and the LGBTQ+ community. It's a great fit for us; the agency has experience matching unusual adoptive parents (in our case, domestic partners) with possibilities outside of the traditional options. This marks the beginning of a two-year journey into the complexities of the adoption process, which includes evaluating our potential as parents, assessing the stability of our home and social environment, and determining how to finance the $40,000 adoption fee, which can increase to $60,000 depending on the birth mother's healthcare expenses.

The entire experience is eye-opening and makes for great, late-night conversations for Jason and me. We crack open a couple of beers and sink down into the puffy couches in our farmhouse living room, with its wide floorboards painted a shiny sky blue, the original wavy glass in the old windows, and our house rabbit Chester bounding and bouncing around the room, and we talk about what kinds of parents we will be. What we will do the same or differently from our own upbringing. The frustration of not being able to begin our family in the old-fashioned way has opened the door to a slower, more methodical approach to parenthood, one that challenges us to look at our lives from the outside, to make us think about what the future could bring and what each of us can do to make it as successful and loving as possible.

The adoption process begins to resemble a job interview, as we transition into crafting a kind of proposal for prospective birth mothers. We have to look as perfect as possible: successful without being too busy, in love without being too obsessive, traditional without being formal, well-rounded but not too quirky. We are required to compile extensive documentation, along with staged photographs of our home (including our empty nursery), endorsements from friends and family, financial statements, and work-related papers.

The agency expresses concerns about how we are coming off—too artistic and free, and our unpredictable schedules, late nights, and frequent travel will raise a red flag for prospective birth mothers. We play down the touring part of our lives, focusing on the university jobs, and I agree to work less and stop touring once the baby arrives, to ensure a stable home environment. It seems to me that there is no way to escape being a woman, that the stereotypes and expectations of a traditional, gendered relationship are fundamental even in the nontraditional agency we have found.

During this same time, I begin to more deeply investigate my fertility problems and start to have hope that I may be able to find a path through my complicated body. We try IUI. After two years, filled with tears, frustrations, enlightenment, and a deep respect and warmth towards that little adoption agency that believes in us, and just shy of signing official adoption papers, I finally have my first successful pregnancy.

I am four days overdue, and I am more than ready. First thing this morning, the midwives perform a membrane sweep to naturally induce labor, which will most likely begin later today. By this point, the weight of the baby feels like a sack of sand I am carrying between my legs, and every bone and muscle in my body aches with tension and anticipation. It is October 19, Jason's birthday, and he is teaching all day at Connecticut College, a lovely campus forty-five minutes from our home. Jason generally doesn't answer his phone (and often doesn't even know where it is, to be supportively honest here), which poses an obvious problem at this particular moment, as I am home alone, and we live an hour away from the hospital where our midwives have privileges. The doula and midwives want me to labor at our house for as long as possible before heading to the hospital. I begin to go into labor late that morning, and I diligently time the length and frequency of my contractions. The doula and Jason will join me when they get to be five minutes apart.

My mother-in-law calls to check in and says she has ordered a delicious cake from a bakery for Jason's birthday, but he's not answering his phone. *No surprise there.* The bakery is only open for another hour, can I pick it up? It's a twenty-five-minute drive from our house. The cake is chocolate and strawberry and they even piped his name on the top. Happy 39th, Jason! During this call, I have to pause for a contraction and mention to my mother-in-law that it's not exactly an ideal time for me because I am alone and in labor. She asks how close the contractions are and laughingly assures me I have plenty of time, and if I just put the driver's seat all the way back, I can get to that bakery and home before I know it. *It's going to be a cake to remember!*

Jason's mom is one of my favorite things about Jason. She was a fearless single mother of two, making ends meet in any way possible. With an independent streak and sense of humor that could crush a bulldozer, she raised Jason into the innate feminist that he is today. She helped him have the humor to laugh through misfortune and always seems to know what to do next, even when those suggestions are illogical or unpractical. When I agree to pick up that cake, I somehow believe she knows something at a deeper level, that this decision is going to help me give birth. It might distract me through an hour of painful contractions and get me moving instead of worrying alone at home.

And so, I drive to the bakery. The steering wheel is nestled in tight against my belly, and I stop twice on the way for some refreshing contractions, pulling over to the side of the road and doing the typical "hee-hee-hoooooooo" breathing, which honestly doesn't seem to do much to ease the internal jackhammering I am currently enjoying. I get to the bakery, and it is as charming as my mother-in-law says. An old, light pink-painted Victorian house with a white swing on the front porch. I squeeze out of the car, waddle up the stairs with my legs in a kind of quarterback stance, gingerly shuffling one foot ahead of the other. As I approach the counter, another contraction hits. I "hee-hee-hoooooooo," and the bakery lunch specials enter my nose in a *most* unwelcome fashion. Is it a meatball sub? A tuna melt? I can already feel the nausea building as I urge the baby to stay put. I hold onto the counter with a slow moan, swaying and closing my eyes, and count through the current contraction. When I look up, two women of about sixty years in age are staring at me wide-eyed. They know exactly what's going on. While they quickly pack up the cake, I call the doula and Jason to tell them to meet me back at the house, leaving a voicemail on Jason's phone as well as several exclamation-filled texts. The bakery ladies suggest nervously that we call an ambulance, but I assure them I have this under control. Five and a half minutes apart and forty-five seconds long. No problem. I grab the cake box and head out, feeling with one hand for the gorgeously wallpapered walls of the front entryway. I throw up in the shrubs on the way to the parking lot, telling the baby to be patient. Tossing the cake (it's a beauty) in the passenger seat, I make it home just as the doula pulls up. By the time we get inside, the contractions are three minutes apart and one minute long. This is progressing fast, and just like that, we hear Jason squealing up the street. The doula grabs my go-bag and the vomit-spattered cake box and we are off.

The rest is a blur, but we do it. Natural childbirth. *Piece of cake!* It is a bit squirrelly at the end, and they lose count of how many stitches they give me. I am ordered to stay in the hospital for three days and on bed rest for three weeks. While they take our little baby to be weighed and examined, I rip open that cake box like a ravenous dinosaur, and, clawing with my hands, I eat in stupendous mouthfuls, delirious with happiness. It certainly remains the most memorable birthday cake I have ever been involved with.

My next concert is six days away. I call our manager from the hospital and tell him in one breath the good news and that I'm not going to be able to make it to that concert. He tells me to buck up, leave the baby with a neighbor, and play the concert like I am contracted to do. I am in terrible pain, am actively bleeding, can't even sit up, and I have to be helped to the toilet. After telling him my situation, he says I am a very resilient young woman and that I can just stand for the concert.

This is the moment I realize I need to make a substantial change in my life. There is no way I am going to convince my manager to evolve. He himself has several grown children who are estranged from him. *Go figure.* Why waste my time or energy on a situation that I will end up running into time and time again? I don't want to slow down in my career, just turn a corner. Fighting against misogyny often feels like punching air. It's millions of tiny particles surrounding everything I do, and I'm pushing back on something impossible to grasp; it's futile. The male bosses hold the marionette strings to my life. *Cut the strings*, I think, and make my own future.

I am planning on a second baby, and I'm not going to be a mother halfway. I have worked this hard to start a family, like I work at everything I have accomplished in my life, and I am damned if I'm not going to figure out how to be the best mother I can possibly be for our baby girl. I hire a substitute violinist for that concert and settle down for my three weeks of baby time. Jason sets up a line of people to come check on me, bring me food, and help me to the bathroom. I continue to bleed heavily for the next week, but I am in good spirits and happy to have this small, wonderful bundle of joy next to me.

Over the next six months, we bring Tzippora with us on tour to over twenty-five states, and I hire babysitters for every city to stay with her backstage when I rehearse and perform. Our manager says he doesn't want the presenters to even have a hint that we have a baby, and I better bring extra dresses in case my milk lets down during a concert. This is the only good advice I get from that insensitive, ridiculous, misogynistic manager. He is in a terrible mood, angry that I gave birth during a busy season, and he tells me if I am planning on having a second baby, I might as well kiss this agency goodbye. Thanks a lot. *And yes*, kiss it goodbye I do.

I take this moment to rethink my life, to recalculate my future. I have always believed in living to the fullest at all moments. This deep-seated, almost instinctual part of me means my life is never stagnant, never boring or without meaning. I take chances every day, often completely unrealistic, sometimes dangerous or silly, and when they go astray, I take it in stride, having already anticipated several directions and solutions. Two backpacking trips through Europe and a couple of solo drives across the country have helped me to think on my feet and find creative solutions to problems on the fly.

I don't believe that a person needs to do the same thing for a long time to harvest the goodness or quality of that activity or profession. Sometimes a thing happens one time and it changes you forever, like a lightning bolt. It seems to me that sometimes people are afraid to leave situations that no longer give them happiness and purpose. Quitting things that don't work for me helps me to stay in the moment, living with joy and challenging me to learn and grow.

For as long as I can remember, I have carried with me the almost visceral knowledge that I can die at any moment. It's a matter-of-fact baseline for me, and it urges me to never be satisfied with a "meh" existence, even for a day. I don't want to regret anything. I want to experience all that the planet and this life have to offer.

This spurs me on, forces me to make quick decisions, work very hard, and embrace learning.

I am an obsessive planner, with a strong stinginess that has me stuffing socks with cash and hiding them around the house. I am never in debt and don't want anyone close to me to be in financial trouble when I die. This way of operating allows me to take risks because I always have a year or more of emergency funds stored up, and I'm completely comfortable living on little income.

After six months of bringing our young daughter on tour with us, I am nearly catatonic with exhaustion. For every stop on our itinerary, I meticulously organize care for her using a paid national service. I read references, review background checks, interview candidates on the phone, and organize detailed schedules. Beyond the normal day-to-day tour details such as travel, car rentals, hotels, rehearsals, social obligations related to the concerts, pre-concert interviews and talks, and the concerts themselves (which have to maintain the highest level), I am breastfeeding, pumping, managing the babysitters, and barely sleeping.

I look ahead at what life will be like in five years, when she will be in school, and I know something has to change. I have friends who have continued as normal with touring, homeschooling their kids, bringing them on the road, or leaving them with a family member or nanny. I'm not interested in this. I have seen those kids hanging out in the back rooms of the concert halls, glued to screens and eating food from vending machines. All alone and miserable. I want a normal childhood for my daughter, with friends and stability.

I plan with my midwives that I will breastfeed for one year, then immediately start the same IUI process again for a second child. Professionally, I have no intention of arguing with our manager or following his insane demands on my personal and professional life. I know that type of career already, have enjoyed it very much, and am ready for the next phase of my life. We have a great situation in Connecticut with a beautiful house and good jobs at universities, and our life can be enough just like that.

Jason and I talk a lot about what we could keep the same or what we could change to make our lives meaningful and enjoyable going forward. He suggests that he could step away from the trio and stay home with the kids while I continue to tour, allowing us to hold on to our current manager and career. But I don't want to play with another cellist. Jason and I have worked for years to build this life together, from competitions in Italy and Germany to festivals from La Jolla to Carnegie Hall. We've studied and learned the core repertoire from incredible mentors, together.

I have spent enough of my musical life accomplishing but not enjoying, and I no longer see a point to that. I've finally found a partner with whom I have both a successful career and a fulfilling relationship. Even when the work is tedious and detailed, like when we spend hours tuning our parts, or working with a metronome, drilling sections, there is always a fun camaraderie, a joke or story to split up the time. People often ask how it can possibly work, living together, working together. But I look forward every day to seeing Jason and sharing our love of music.

I propose something radical. Put our careers on the back burner; just play a couple of concerts a year to keep our name active. Quit our jobs. Sell our house. Move across the country to the small town of Corvallis, Oregon, an idealistic and beautiful place nestled in the Willamette Valley, forty-five minutes from the wild and magnificent coast and ninety minutes from the majestic peaks of the Cascade Range. Jason's family is nearby, and over the course of several tours through the Pacific Northwest, we have always stopped to perform and teach in Corvallis. I adore this town and somehow have managed to make deeper connections there than I have in all our years in Connecticut. I have enough money saved up for us to take the chance and get set up in a new place and I want a beautiful and friendly town to raise our family.

We put our house on the market, pack our things, and head west. I contact all of the universities within two hours of Corvallis and we both find adjunct positions. Jason gets a job as the conductor of the Eugene Youth Orchestra. I find a house for rent online, sign the lease, and we are off!

I am looking for ways to stay connected professionally, and two concertmaster openings pop up. The first is Portland Opera, an opportunity for me to learn a new kind of repertoire and style of playing. I practice like a maniac, have some online lessons with friends who are members of opera orchestras, and take the audition. It has been common practice for the past several decades to have orchestral auditions behind a screen, with a carpeted floor and no speaking allowed to hide the gender and identity of the player. This is the case for Portland Opera, and I am so pleased to be offered a two-year position as leader of the orchestra. It is challenging, supportive, and the productions are magnificent in their scope and passion.

I begin to try to get pregnant with our second child. Although the IUI process is familiar, it is no less difficult to retain a pregnancy than the first time.

Four months later, a second concertmaster position opens. A reputable symphony fairly close to home needs someone to fill a one-year position. *Fantastic!* For this audition, the first round is behind a screen, but the finals are open, on the big stage, with a panel of adjudicators spread through the audience. Concertmaster auditions are incredibly stressful, with a large amount of repertoire including two major concertos, orchestral excerpts, and demanding concertmaster solos. I am confident. I have worked hard for this day and am solidly prepared. The committee is pleasant, asking me questions between the selections, or requesting I play the excerpt again in a different tempo or mood.

And then, a voice from the audience. I can make out the conductor, a large, solid man in his early middle-age. With a booming voice, he asks, "Are you pregnant?" Is there no end to what a woman has to deal with to have a career? It isn't the time to point out the fact that it is illegal to ask that question in a job interview. I simply say, "Yes, early days yet, but yes." After which, he continues his line of questioning to ask me what my plans are during the pregnancy and after. I answer honestly, and after that, play the shit out of the rest of my audition. They call me later that day to offer me the job.

These next five years of our lives are amazing. Everything I dream of and more. Our old Craftsman house overflows with students and friends; we can walk to more bakeries than I can list on one hand; and we buy a beautiful vacation house on the coast in an eco-community, which we can rent out to supplement our income and where we spend weekends and holidays. I have the calmness, space, and happiness to have a successful second pregnancy and to raise our two little girls.

My goal of continuing my career while raising a family in a beautiful place close to Jason's family and without the obligation to spend nights away from home or to travel great distances is realized. I settle in to be a mom, not anticipating that in five short years, we will be living in the heart of Berlin, Germany.

❧ 5

Home Alone

It's tight in here, under my sweaters and topped with a heavy lap blanket. It's hard to breathe, but if I keep a steady in and out, and make a little cave by my nose and mouth with my hands, I can stay in here *forever.* The wooden slats on the side of the trunk have little spaces between them and I can see light and shadow through the cracks. One of the best things about this place is that it is fast to get to and doesn't seem, to someone out there looking, like a big enough place for a six-year-old to fit. So it's good, if I have enough time to put the sweaters and blanket back, making sure that the metal clasp on the antique wooden trunk closes quiet and tight. I am always careful to lower the lid really slowly, feeling with my fingers as I shut the trunk on top of me, checking to see there is no blanket poking out, because I don't want him to see anything and I know he will come looking for me soon.

I can still hear the muffled screaming in the kitchen eating nook, with the regular accompaniment of crashing things, hysterical arguments, and crying. I've been through this before; not sure how many times exactly, but enough for me to know the routine. It will go on for probably another twenty minutes, then there will be a diminuendo, a tense silence for several minutes, then my two older sisters running upstairs, followed by my father calling my name:

"Sarah, you get in here right this instant. I'm going to count to ten, and if you aren't here by then, there's going to be big trouble."

That's part of the reason I changed my name to Anthea after I left home. I just can't stop that instinctual terror-filled shiver every time I hear someone call me by that name.

Eventually, his voice and footsteps come up the stairs, the same stairs you see in the opening of the movie *Home Alone*, which has its own kind of family dysfunction, but in a cheery, loving way. In *our Home Alone*, my father storms out of the kitchen, comes into the front hallway, stomps up the stairs with that charming, curved banister, and bursts into my room. I can only see the shadow of his feet, but I can still hear his heavy breathing, as if he has just sprinted around the block (I suppose hitting children is a type of aerobic activity) and see his reddened face in my mind's eye. His favorite methods are belt and the thick wooden cutting board that has a handy attached handle, the one that is used every day to prepare meals. But then one day he will break that in half over my sister's fragile body, one of those times when I am forced to watch and wait my turn, when I can't find a chance to escape.

Inside my trunk, I am familiar with that voice and how he looks when he uses it. My heart thumps so hard it feels like he will be able to hear it outside my trunk but he doesn't find me. He never does. I have four solid spots that I rotate between, depending on how much time I think I have. You can see his rages coming, his comments accelerating, sentences tightening and quickening. Face starting to swell and redden, eyes receding and hands starting to activate. Slapping on the table, hitting the arm of his chair. There is no reasoning. But there *is* an arc. After about forty-five minutes, I emerge from my spot, begin to practice, and he might pop his head in a bit later and say, "Goodnight, kiddo, sounding good!"

And that is that.

This violent era of my childhood is only at its zenith for a couple of years, from the moment my grandfather dies when I am six to when our family hires a live-in maid when I am eight. We move to Winnetka, Illinois, a wealthy suburb of Chicago, the winter my grandfather dies. For us, being home alone as a family is *very* dangerous. If just one person is added to the mix, my father controls his rages, presenting a perfect picture to any outsiders.

My oldest sister runs away from home at age sixteen, the day after an episode where I thought he might actually kill her, and soon after that my mother discovers that my father has burned through a huge swath of the inheritance she received from my grandfather.

My mother makes a change that summer; she takes over the finances, gets a job, and starts to loosely protect her children. I ask her once if Dad ever hits her, and she replies, "Goodness no, I would leave in a heartbeat if he did!" This cements my instinctual understanding that she is not an ally. She works for the other side. It is each person for themselves here.

There is, however, a saving grace at this moment of epiphany for my mother: she hires Agnieszka, a recent Polish immigrant, to come stay with us as our live-in maid, and thus my father's tirades can only happen on weekends from then on. Agnieszka is as kind as can be, generous, has a soft, enveloping hug, and understands children. She protects me, gives me all of the warmth I had been missing, and lets me be free inside my own home.

Agnieszka stays with her brother and niece on the weekends, creating a more stable rhythm for our family. Things can only get really dangerous while she is gone. We are all busy on the weekends anyway, with youth orchestra, lessons, and chamber music rehearsals, so scheduling his tirades into those small windows between Saturday morning and Sunday evening becomes difficult for my father.

My trunk is one of three matching ones my mother found at an antique store, and all through my childhood it sits at the end of my bed, also an antique. As adults, both of my sisters still have their trunks, and my mother puzzles over why I don't want mine when she offers it to me. It certainly is beautiful, made from a dark burnished wood, the wide slats showing its history. About two feet wide, the top is curved like the swollen belly of a cow, and flint-gray metal strips wind around it, both horizontally and vertically. I can't even look at that gorgeous piece of furniture without a cold, sharp shiver involuntarily zipping through my body.

Our house is furnished entirely with antiques, which makes everything feel formal, or as if I am a visitor. My room is covered with hand-painted French wallpaper, with vertical lines of mint green leaves spaced one inch apart, minuscule blush pink roses intertwining. I stare at that wallpaper, imagining a person with their tiny brush painting every single one of those flowers. We aren't allowed to hang anything of our own on the walls, certainly never use tape or nails. My bed is a raised full-sized, with white wrought iron foot- and headboard, a wooden step stool with three steps for me to reach the bed, a lace bed skirt, and a handmade coverlet that perfectly complements the color scheme of the room. I have a matching doll bed, with the same wrought iron and bedspread, where "Little Susie" lives, a muslin hand-stitched doll in a charming pilgrim dress, apron, and bonnet.

One of my favorite pieces in the room is a white dressing table with a large, beveled mirror and a cushioned stool that tucks beneath the skirted arms. These arms open wide, with their white, floor-length lace hanging below, to reveal a long, thin drawer where I can keep all of my little things. We can't have anything on the surfaces of our tables, bed, or floor, and the closets are equally maintained.

My father, who is quite handy, lines my closet with cedar, putting in shelves for pants and shoes. This is my *least* favorite place to hide, my fourth spot, because it is so easily exposed and close to the action, but it works if I have no time. I can squeeze on top of the shoe shelves, behind the hanging shirts, thanking my dad for unwittingly building me this hiding spot, and when he comes looking for me, he pushes against the clothes to see if I am there. I can feel his large hands pressing against me, but I melt into the corner and somehow, in his frantic, altered state, he can't find me. My whole body cramps up from balancing on that shelf, but it is a good, solid option.

It's only recently that I have begun telling people that I grew up in the *Home Alone* house. It's unnerving to smile and answer questions about it, fighting down my memories. It was years before I even had the guts to watch the movie. I intended to watch it again before writing this chapter, but I couldn't find the right moment. I would have to be alone, undisturbed. I was by myself, on tour, typing the beginnings of the chapter on my iPhone, grabbing a bite to eat before heading to the airport for my flight home. I could download *Home Alone* to watch on the plane, but I was afraid I might need space, might have one of those post-traumatic stress attacks I get occasionally, which have lessened since I cut off contact with my father thirteen years ago. I could watch the movie later in the week—but I didn't want to risk it. I don't want to bother Jason with my baggage. It's all still *too close.*

John Hughes, the director, actually used the inside and outside of our house, my street, and my neighbors' houses in the movie. The street was blocked off for months. They change certain things in our house, like making the basement scary instead of our normal basement, with the ping-pong table, air hockey, pool table, Atari, and my dad's offices. And they change the wallpaper and furniture, change the third floor, where my oldest sister and then later Agnieszka lived. But I can still see my room, the kitchen, the banister. And it's such a fun, exuberant movie, based on mutual love and hilarity, the house looking messy and lived in. The opposite of our home.

My parents sell the house when my next older sister goes to college, buying a smaller house about a mile away. Sometimes I walk over to the house and watch the filming, the guys whose whole jobs are to make sure no one steps on the fresh snow, the trucks lining the street just out of view, the crew stomping their feet to stay warm, cupping coffee in their gloved hands.

𝄐

At age six, I am already an accomplished violinist. I wouldn't say child prodigy, but certainly precocious, hardworking, and because of my two amazing older sisters and mother, the Kreston name carries a certain weight, music-wise, in the Chicago area and beyond.

Being a classical violinist means that you spend hour upon hour alone, practicing, thinking, feeling. It was and is the perfect escape for me, for who would disturb a person of any age working diligently and carefully alone in their room for hour upon hour? I am, in this way, often alone inside my own home from a very early age, and my violin, as it does time and time again in my life, saves me, protects me, and offers me a path away from danger and towards happiness and fulfillment.

That 10,000-hour mark that Malcolm Gladwell says you have to achieve to reach a level of mastery on a subject? That's nothing to a serious classical musician. That won't even darken the door of a top-level music school or put your name in the running to solo with an orchestra or get management. That's child's play.

I have a grainy photograph from the summer of 1975. It's me, age two, with my unruly auburn hair perfectly parted in the middle, two huge, round ponytails held by mismatched blue and clear bubble hair ties, with a halo of fuzzy renegade curls popping out at irregular angles. My blue and white gingham summer dress, with floral paneling and white lace trim, has a name tag stuck to the front, which lends a little perspective, because it covers half of the front of my tiny dress. My pudgy hands are holding a backwards black violin case, which also has what looks to be an enormous name tag on it. I am half-squinting, half-smiling at the person taking the photo, probably my mother. It is the summer I start violin, on a 1/64th-sized instrument, a ridiculously small violin that can fit in a handbag. On a good day it sounds like a gnat stuck inside a balloon. But for me it is a perfect fit. And it is *all mine.*

Have you held the hand of a two-year-old child recently? Warm, soft, with teeny little fingernails. The infant palmar reflex, that instinct to grab anything put into their small hands, seems to still be there; they hold tight as they grasp your hand to cross the street. Officially toddlers, they can now hop on one foot and may be able to name the colors of the rainbow. Famous for being petite divas and often clad in diapers, some two-year-olds—as impossible as it seems—can even play the violin.

I am two and a half when I first attend the American Suzuki Institute in Stevens Point, Wisconsin—a family-oriented summer camp on the campus of the University of Wisconsin and one of the largest events of its kind in the United States. Big, ugly blocks of buildings connected by concrete walkways.

We drive up from Chicago: Mom, me, and my two older sisters, who are already quite amazing performers (aged six, a cellist, and ten, a violinist). My teacher has impossibly fluffy orange hair, like cotton candy piled on top of her head. Each of us has daily private lessons, group classes according to age and level, and performs in the evening concerts.

These events are massive, held in the big gym at the university. They go something like this: a tsunami of identically dressed children, all playing the same piece at the same time, with a teacher leading them and a piano pounding out the accompaniment. The front row is the tiniest of students, stretching across the stage, wiggling, jiggling, scratching, and doing their best to remember what they are supposed to be doing. The tiers of students grow taller towards the back of the stage.

Starting with that old chestnut "Twinkle Variations," one learns more and more difficult selections. There are ten Suzuki volumes of progressively more challenging pieces. After each set of pieces, groups of children exit the stage, having completed what they can play. At the end of these interminably long and boring concerts, only a couple of students remain standing, playing the most advanced pieces, again with identical movements and fingerings. It is like slo-mo *Survivor*, but with a costume department recruited from the local Catholic boarding school and none of the excitement of eating live spiders. The musicians on stage sound just as identical as they look. Once I am done with the pieces I know, I sit with my mother on a metal folding chair for what feels like seven years. I guess that is part of the training, though. Teaching stillness, patience, and observation. It is all worth it for the chance to stand in front of that monstrous, humming silver rectangle in the cafeteria that dispenses chocolate or vanilla ice cream into and over my cone at the end of every dinner.

The Suzuki Method is taught with the "mother tongue" philosophy, where the child learns not by reading sheet music, but by imitation of the teacher and daily listening to Suzuki-produced recordings, again with the performer playing exactly the same markings and tempi that the student will imitate. It takes me an entire year to master "Twinkle," and I can't even imagine how tedious and annoying it must have been for my parents to hear that every day, for an hour, squeaking out of my ridiculously small violin. Not to mention how boring it must have been for me. I mean, that's more than five hundred hours of "Twinkle," between the lessons, practicing, and listening to that lifeless, unimaginative recording.

The official Suzuki violin recordings I'd heard so

often were recently pulled from production because the violinist I grew up listening to, who, when I was a teenager studying from him at summer camp, would rest his hand on my lower back while I was playing, was accused of sexual misconduct. The recordings were remade by Hilary Hahn, a shining beacon of goodness with a heart of gold.

My first summer camp must have gone pretty well because I continue private lessons and group class during the year in Chicago. I practice daily with my dad, who takes over the lesson prep because my mother has her hands full with my older sisters and their myriad activities. Eventually he gives up learning violin alongside me because I am progressing faster than he can keep up with. He happily brings me to the lessons and supports me but can't manage to get his fingers to cooperate once we have to begin playing more than one note at a time.

Dr. Suzuki himself, aged seventy-seven at the time, comes to Chicago in 1977, when I am four. I am one of a handful of young violinists selected from the Chicago area to play for him, which is a huge honor. We are lined up, in our official Suzuki Method outfits (navy bottoms and white button-down shirts). When Dr. Suzuki arrives at the O'Hare Airport, a delegation of teachers greets him, and each of the violinists plays a solo from one of his books for him, right in the airport. I can't remember what I played, but I do remember the feeling of standing still for a long time, the red carpet I stood on, my shiny black shoes, and the feeling of being very small and alone in a big, cold room. Dr. Suzuki has a slim, slightly hunched frame, gray suit, gentle smile, and patient gaze. After the presentations he comes down the row of performers, and after we bow to one another, he holds my small hand in between his cold, leathery ones and thanks me in his soft, steady voice.

For the Suzuki Method, the parent has to be very involved. Teachers often have the parent sign a contract promising to practice with the child for one hour a day. For me, the Suzuki Method is a great starting point, a way to embrace hard work, but it does nothing to foster my own creativity. It does reinforce a fierce competitive streak in me, as I am able to quickly progress through the books, proudly letting people know which book and piece I have just finished. I can't really read music. I can just play like everyone else. Exactly like everyone else.

Two years after meeting Dr. Suzuki, we move to Winnetka, Illinois, so that my oldest sister can be part of a stronger public high school music program. I move from a 1/64th violin through the 1/32nd, the 1/16th, and finally to the 1/8th. Bigger sound each time my instrument gets bigger. More possibilities. And I move away from the Suzuki Method. My new teacher is Dr. Goldberg, and he shows me the traditional European style of playing. A romantic, full-bodied, expressive repertoire that I am eager to explore. I am ready to find out who I am, how I feel, and how to show that to the world.

I can still picture Dr. Goldberg's looping, old-fashioned cursive writing on ancient sheet music. He passed in 2002, and I had the good fortune of being well-enough remembered by him, even all of those years later, that several boxes of his music library were given to me. Old, funny editions, heavily edited by hand with his specific verbiage, unique markings, and extra flourishes—arrows up or down to indicate intonation, expressive directions such as "deep sadness here" or "a spring day."

The music itself has the texture of a papadum, that crisp and thin lentil cracker given as an appetizer in

Indian restaurants. Bend it much beyond flat and the whole sheet of music will snap in half from the brittleness of age. The manuscript spines have old brown string hanging out, and they have a distinctly musty smell and must be stored lying down for fear of total disintegration.

Dr. Goldberg seems impossibly old to six-year-old me. I can't tell the difference between his wife and mother, who share his tiny house. Both are robustly built, a contrast to Dr. Goldberg's pencil-thin frame. Their hair is always covered by a scarf, they walk with a heavy, stiff gait, chat in an unknown language, and they bustle. If there is ever a perfect representation of bustle, it was the Mrs. Goldbergs. There is a lot of wiping of the hands on their aprons and poofs of flour. Strange, strong, exotic smells and crackling sounds of meat being cooked waft into the teaching room, which doubles as the eating area after lessons are complete; a small table covered by handmade lace with a thick plastic sheet over it, set for three places.

Dr. Goldberg is from a Russian/Lithuanian family who had run a small general store in Chicago, and he walks with a noticeable limp, a vestige of his childhood polio. He had spent much of his childhood bedridden, practicing violin, and it became clear that music would make a suitable career. He went on to teach band and orchestra in the public schools, and he never tires of furthering himself, earning a doctorate, warming up with Paganini *Caprices* and Vieuxtemps. He is famous for his 4th of July performances in our town parade, where he would play the impossibly difficult "Yankee-Doodle" variations with flags sticking out of his outfit. Every year, before our summer break, he allows me to ride once up and down his stairway elevator chair, a terribly slow ride, but traveling sideways up a staircase and getting a glimpse into the privacy of their diminutive second floor is something I look forward to all year long.

I take lessons from him only for two years, as he lovingly and patiently transitions me from my Suzuki training to a traditional European approach. Dr. Goldberg teaches from Wohlfahrt, Ševčík, and *Introducing the Positions*—all incredibly tedious technical methods that are the bread and butter of serious violinists throughout the world. He is patient and kind, thoughtful and quiet, exacting. There are no stickers or practice charts like I had with Suzuki. There is work to be done, and heavy expectations. He is unforgiving with his demands on the position of my hands and wrists, left-hand double-stop finger preparations. I don't know at the time how advanced these techniques are. Especially for a six- to eight-year-old. He speaks to me as an adult, explaining, forming and holding my hands (even when painful), and expecting clear improvement from week to week. I am always up for a challenge and relish showing off in public performance, my lion's mane of curly red hair flying around as I play my small violin. By the end of our time together, working on Mozart's *Violin Concerto No. 3*, he knows I will be moving on.

And I do, from a 1/8th-sized violin to a 1/4th and 1/2, and to my next teachers, an incredible husband and wife team originally from New York. Almita and Roland Vamos, of Hungarian and Russian descent, two of the most revered pedagogues in the United States. They train formidable superstars, winners of international competitions, leaders of major orchestras and chamber music groups, and soloists. I am fortunate to get a coveted space in their studio. While most eight-year-olds are enjoying the freedom of childhood, I am spending more and more time alone practicing, meticulous and self-critical. Observing, crafting, and digging deep into a determination which carries me to this day.

It is during a bucolic summer vacation in our family's second home in Green Lake, Wisconsin, a three-hour drive north of Chicago, that the final straw breaks for my oldest sister. I always look forward to spending time in Green Lake, which holds many wonderful memories of my grandfather and where I get to branch out and explore by myself. As often as we can, one of us three girls invites a friend to join us for the trip, the guest providing that cushion of safety around any potential tantrums from my father. On this occasion, however, we are alone.

I am getting ready for a summer music camp in the Adirondacks in New York. It will be hours of supervised practice every day, with lessons, master classes, and recitals. I am eight years old. It will be my first summer studying with my new teachers at Meadowmount School of Music. These teachers offered all of their students a safe haven, both physically—in my case, and for my oldest sister when she attended the camp—and through dedication, hard work, and self-discovery through music.

Our family's vacation house is on a lake in central Wisconsin. It's a fifteen-minute drive from our other vacation property, an eighty-acre farm. Both of these properties were purchased by E.B. before I was born. We spend our time alternately around the fireplace, ice-skating, cross-country skiing, going to the flea market, swimming in the lake, having sailing lessons, waterskiing, and taking the golf cart out for massive adventures. Our house is situated within the American Baptist Assembly, a large, gated estate that has a hotel, conference spaces, a golf course, a pool and recreation building, and a number of large, private homes.

My grandfather liked to golf, and behind our house is another building that we call "Las Vegas" because my grandfather won enough money one weekend in Vegas to build the little house and furnish it with his own three-wheeled, fringed golf cart. We spend a lot of time in that cart, exploring the grounds. E.B. taught me to drive. By age five, I am taking the cart out by myself, packing a sandwich and blanket in the back, and getting lost along the twisting roads. If I "run out of juice," I walk until I find a house, knock on the door, tell them I'm E.B.'s granddaughter, and they'll call him. He'll show up some time later, in his light blue Lincoln Continental convertible, tie a rope around the golf cart, and tow us back to Las Vegas to get plugged in.

I'm not sure what tips my dad over the edge that weekend the summer when I am eight, but my sister had already known that she was in danger, that she needed to leave. Although she is eight years older than me, she and I have always shared some kind of deep trust and understanding about our childhood. She takes me aside for a walk, and asks if she can have my help in an important mission.

She is going to leave for good the next day and go to Western Illinois University (where our violin teachers are professors) and start a new life. She thinks that if she can get far enough away, my father can't or won't catch her. Her plan is detailed and excellent, and I agree without hesitation that this has to be her next step. I am honored to be her accomplice and to know that she trusts me. She has a bus ticket from the town of Green Lake, three miles down the lake from us, which will get her to Milwaukee, then she will take a train through Chicago to Macomb, Illinois. Her friend will pick her up there, and my sister will work as cleaning crew at the dorms to pay for food and housing. The university has admitted her on full merit scholarship for violin performance. The two teenage boys down the lane from our vacation house will drive her in their boat to Green Lake at six in the morning, and she needs a decoy to throw my parents off the track long enough for her to get on that bus. She will wake me up at five, and I should drive the golf cart to the Baptist Assembly recreation center, parking it off to one side, and then come back home by foot, as fast as possible, and go back to sleep.

This plan works like a charm, and by the time our parents realize she's gone, it is too late. They notice the missing golf cart, violin, and clothes, and my dad decides to drive around the grounds to look for the cart. I innocently offer to go along as his wing man. We drive around, and I "spot" our golf cart to the side of the recreation building. My dad goes in to ask after my sister. He is properly thrown off the track, my sister has a successful escape, and I see her here and there over the next eight years that I live with my parents. Her timing is perfect, because what had happened the evening before, in my eyes, was one of the most frightening episodes I have been a part of.

I'm not sure what escalates it, and really, there is no rhyme or reason to my father's irrational, uncontrollable temper. But at the end of his evening tirade, I am hiding behind the curved couch, and my dad picks up a large, beautiful wingback chair, with carved wooden legs and a cream and light green patterned upholstery, and throws it across the room, barely missing my sister, who dives for cover. The chair splinters against the wall, one back leg broken clean off, and my sister runs from the house.

It is time for her to go. And she has the plan to do it. From then on, that chair sits propped up against a corner in the basement, the broken leg lying just under the off-kilter chair. I don't know why no one throws it away or tries to fix it, just leaving it as is, as if it will somehow fix itself someday and walk up the stairs to rejoin the rest of the matching furniture in the living room.

I know my mother is sad to have lost her oldest daughter, but she rarely shows her emotions or shares her feelings. *Stoic. Well-mannered. Polite.* So when I go into the garage the next week and see her behind the wheel of my grandfather's old Lincoln Continental, a car which we rarely use anymore, with her head resting on the wheel, I quietly open the passenger door and step inside. She is silently sobbing, and I put my hand on her shoulder. It all pours out. She feels alone, with no parents or family. She is overwhelmed and knows my father's behavior is wrong but doesn't know any better way of "controlling" us. He has spent a huge amount of her inheritance, was in big trouble with the IRS, the finances are in shambles, he has been lying and hasn't made money in years, they are going to have to sell my grandfather's warehouse. Luckily, the *Home Alone* house was paid for in cash by my grandfather. She is going to have to get a job. She isn't strong enough to leave, she's going to try to fix it. I had never seen her cry, let alone lose even a sliver of her perfect composure. But she is fully crying now, her shoulders heaving. She is going to drive to her parents' graves, and I will go along.

Fifteen minutes later, we turn in to the Green Lake cemetery, a place we visit regularly to maintain the graves, planting flowers and wiping down the gravestones. We pull to the side of the lane, and my mother kneels when we come to the two stones. She stays there for a long time as I wander around the cemetery, reading gravestones and generally being an eight-year-old. At the head of our family plot are two tall, healthy cypress trees that reach towards the sky. Below them, I see something moving in the grass, making small painful sounds. As I approach on my hands and knees, I see that it is a baby robin with a broken wing and with something wrong with its leg.

I take off my outer shirt and, gently wrapping the bird inside, go back to find my mother. She has collected herself and, with red-rimmed eyes, says she is happy to have my company. I show her my bird, and she says we can take it home and help it to regain its health so it can return to the wild.

Over the next week, we take care of that little bird together, crushing boiled eggs to feed it, keeping it warm in a shoebox lined with old rags. And by the end of the week, it is ready to fly away. We open the box on the lawn, gently tip it to the side, and watch the little bird totter and take a couple of bouncing steps before it takes flight. I look at my mother, hoping that our next steps will somehow also be this good, that we will be able to heal and start in a new direction.

𝄐

After all these years, I suppose I could just forgive him, which is what he has asked for, in an insincere and condescending way. But I can never let him be around my children. He will not know them. Abuse is a disease that spreads well past the immediate people involved. It spreads to their partners, to their children and grandchildren, making everyone second-guess their behaviors, hide things, lie, not knowing the right way to act or react.

When Jason and I were so desperate to have children, after we had tried for years, gone to the doctors, and were working through the tremendously frustrating and tedious adoption process, which seemed dead set against us, saving and scrimping to afford the baby we both fiercely wanted, we ran into one more wall. The question came up on one of the endless forms. Have you ever been the victim of child abuse? The truth is that if I told the truth, we would not be eligible to adopt a child. I had to lie. I had to cover up his selfish, stupid, childish behavior *once again*. Not only for myself or him this time, but also for the man I loved and the child we wanted to love together. That is, to me, unforgivable.

※ 6
Silk Road

It's a large assault rifle; I'm pretty sure an AK-47, but what do I know, apart from watching James Bond movies or the random John le Carré flick. A curved magazine hanging down from the disturbingly worn stock, an oversized shoulder butt, and a handy strap for carrying it around town, or the compound, or I guess wherever you might need such an appendage. It's larger than I had imagined one would be, taking up the entire white stone windowsill, the breeze from the garden pushing the thin white curtains into the room through the open windows. I am in Central Asia, on tour with Yo-Yo Ma, and every moment of this trip, from the security briefing in New York City, from the private airplane to the chunks of horsemeat served on thin scimitars, the sweaty discotheques, the myriad translators, the warlords, and the epic storyteller in a trance chanting ancient texts, feels like a tangible dream.

I walk tentatively across the room, an oversized bedroom sumptuously decorated with bold, brightly patterned yak-wool tapestries, short round wooden tables with intricately carved scenes, and striking textured cushions on the floor. The private bath is covered with teeny multicolored ceramic tiles and miniature framed paintings depicting people sitting in a room very similar to the one I am currently in. Leaning over the Kalashnikov, I peer out the window. There is a guard with his back towards me, wearing a long, dark woolen army coat, and relieving himself on a beautifully maintained shrub in the ornamental garden along the side of the whitewashed building. Turning around, he walks confidently towards me and grabs his gun, grunting something in Kazakh.

I am the guest of a wealthy family who owns this compound surrounded by a high wall with barbed wire, armed guards, extensive gardens, a large main residence, and many outbuildings for various purposes. They have enough extra space and staff to house and feed our entire entourage of around fifty people.

A couple of years earlier, Jason and I had been lucky enough to be part of the initial exploration of a new project by the cellist Yo-Yo Ma, held in the utopian beauty of Tanglewood. Nestled in the rolling verdant hills of the Berkshire Mountains of Western Massachusetts, Tanglewood is the summer home of the Boston Symphony Orchestra and one of the most important music venues and training schools in North America. State-of-the-art concert halls of various sizes dot the green expanse, with older wooden buildings serving as rehearsal and educational spaces. It's the year 2000.

I am living in Hartford, Connecticut. Jason, who I have recently begun dating, moves up from New York City to join my quartet, the Avalon String Quartet, as the new cellist. We decide to live together, squeezing into my teeny apartment on the top floor of a house in a rather sketchy part of the city. The ceilings are so short that he can only stand up in the exact middle of the main room. The kitchen is just a sink, mini-fridge, and hot plate; the bathroom feels like one of those diminutive bathrooms in an old RV; and there is only one heating vent in the whole place. In the winter, we wake in the mornings absolutely freezing, seeing our breath in puffs coming out of each other's mouths. My lovebird, Aphrodite, climbs down from her cage, patters across the room, and, using her beak for leverage, scales the mattress, standing proudly puffed up as close to my face as she can get. Chirping at the top of her lungs to wake me up, I can feel her two little feet on me, bouncing like she is doing miniature jumping jacks with every mighty squeak.

I am halfway through my master's degree in violin performance from the Hartt School of Music at the University of Hartford, where my quartet is in residence with the renowned Emerson String Quartet. In the Avalon Quartet, though, I am the violist, not a violinist. I'm one of that rare breed of musicians who can play both violin and viola equally well. A musical switch-hitter. On viola I inhabit the role of an "inner voice," a bridge between the bright sound of the violins and the deep, rich sonority of the cello.

We have worked our way up in the past three years, studying for a year with members of the Cleveland Quartet, then two years at Northern Illinois University with the Vermeer Quartet, and now have landed a coveted residency with the Emerson Quartet.

We attend summer festivals, actively tour, and have started to win some major competitions. Our stipends from the school make it possible for us to dedicate ourselves to the art of string quartet playing full-time. Our schedule includes intense weekly quartet lessons with the Emersons, a minimum of four hours of quartet practice a day, plus several hours of personal practice.

I decide to take advantage of the free degree the school offers to me, which adds a full load of classwork on top of my quartet residency obligations. I am busy up to my eyeballs with school, and the trio I had started the year before with Jason and a stellar pianist is unexpectedly taking wing. We get management and are invited by the legendary violinist Isaac Stern to spend three weeks, all expenses paid, in New York, working with him at Carnegie Hall. I am juggling two groups, two instruments, a serious relationship, three animals, and a degree on top of it. *Just my style.*

That first summer in Hartford, I get a call. Yo-Yo Ma is inviting Jason and me to be part of an amazing new initiative called the Silk Road Project. Yo-Yo, in addition to being one of the greatest performers alive, has the ability to communicate and collaborate with basically any living thing. Ninety-two albums, nineteen Grammys, performances with every major orchestra on the planet, United Nations Messenger of Peace, French-American child prodigy born to Chinese parents and educated at Juilliard and Harvard. When he is on stage, it feels like he is playing straight into your heart, and any one of the thousands of people in the audience would say exactly the same thing. He collaborates across genres with artists such as Sting and Carlos Santana, and effortlessly plays with bluegrass, tango, and folk musicians. He is in the *New York Times* crossword puzzle, mentioned on *Seinfeld*. And his team calls me.

I simply cannot tell you how excited I am, it's not even possible. It is like a pair of giant hands descend from the clouds, scoop me up, and whisper in my ear that I am to have all my wishes come true. *I am grinning so deeply it feels like I am cleaved in two.*

Yo-Yo brings together a group of one hundred people.

We are here to explore music from the Silk Road, Eastern and Western classical musicians working together on newly composed music. All of Tanglewood is abuzz with historians, composers, patrons, performers from India, Japan, Azerbaijan, Armenia, Pakistan, and more, with a slew of translators. The biggest names in performance from many cultures are there, playing traditional instruments such as the Persian kemanche, the Chinese zheng, Indian tabla, even a Mongolian singer. Top-drawer composers join the group as well as Yo-Yo's high-powered management team. And a hand-selected group of twenty-five young Western musicians. He asks Carnegie Hall for some recommendations. Isaac Stern, who is a close friend of Yo-Yo, has taken a shine to our trio at his Carnegie program and thinks Jason and I will be a good fit.

Despite how bigger than life Yo-Yo Ma is, being around him feels intimate, wondrous, precious. When I first meet him, what strikes me is how unassuming he is. He is a couple of inches shorter than I am and is wearing everyday slacks and a button-down shirt. He could be anyone. You wouldn't pick him out at the grocery store as an exceptional human, just a dad out shopping for his weekly staples. But he has a remarkable aura, both calm and massive. He is quiet, thoughtful, always observing and listening. Being in his presence is the closest I have ever gotten to something that permeates you the way I imagine a magical or supernatural being might.

There is something about playing classical violin, a style of music that has no words, has no descriptive directives beyond approximate speed, volume, rhythm, and pitch, that forces you to reach beyond basic human emotions. The notes on the page are a gateway into the mind and heart of the person who wrote them down, regardless of how long ago that was, what language or culture that human came from. Coming together with these musicians from all over the world, who don't share a language, not even a common tablature or agreement on what pitch or rhythm is, frees us to a degree beyond what any of us has ever experienced.

Written music is completely different from one tradition to another. Chinese notation has lists of numbers which correspond to which finger is to be used on which string and for how long. It mainly uses the pentatonic scale, only five notes per octave, like using only the black keys on a piano, and has many types of slides and expressive, almost vocal glissandos between notes. Western classical musical notation has staves of five lines, twenty-four different keys, twelve notes per octave, specific notations for rhythms, and several clefs which are used for different pitch ranges. Indian and Middle Eastern music uses microtones, meaning instead of twelve equal intervals per octave like there are in Western classical music, they have many more. The notes that exist between the keys of a piano keyboard. Several of the musicians at Tanglewood come from a completely oral tradition with no written music whatsoever.

That week in Tanglewood, all of my classical training is turned on its head. I quickly begin to learn to play microtones, Szechuan Opera, and improvise in different styles. I throw myself into it, attending as many activities beyond the rehearsals and performances as I can. I love hearing the historians of different cultures explain the origins of our stringed instruments, tracing them back one thousand years to the Chinese erhu, a two-stringed violin covered in python skin, and back even further to the kemanche, a Persian violin with a history of two thousand years, made from a hollowed-out gourd.

I had always been taught in school that the violin was invented in Italy in the mid-1500s by the great master builders such as Amati and later Stradivarius. This kind of Eurocentric version of history is technically accurate, but also quite wrong. I am excited to learn that the Chinese and Persian violins had been traded along the Silk Road hundreds of years before Stradivarius even existed. It was a sort of incidental trade; the traders carried the Asian violins with them as small and portable entertainment systems, like cowboys slinging their guitars over their backs or tucking a harmonica into their vest pockets. Something to while away the evening hours around the campsite after you had watered and brushed your camel.

I feel pretty intimidated by the level of musicians at Tanglewood, especially the Western musicians my age. Most have attended Juilliard or Curtis, have solo careers, have won international competitions, and even have recordings out. It's clear to me that I am outgunned. I have more or less thrown away three years of my life having an extended meltdown and feel like I have fallen off the road that I had been on since I was two years old. While these musicians were entering big solo competitions, I was smoking pot, playing in a band, and getting a Women's Studies degree.

I swallow my fear and feelings of inadequacy and delve into the experience. I try to imitate the sounds of these radical and exotic instruments, incorporating new slides, colors, and techniques into my playing. I am here because someone believes in me, and I am pretty much as open to anything as possible at this point, thanks to my patchwork education and varied life experiences. Not only the discipline of rigorous, old-school training, but years of throwing all of that right out the window in search of greater, or anyway, *different*, meaning.

I love every minute of it, and perhaps that's what Yo-Yo sees in me, because as the Silk Road Project begins to take shape, I am honored to be one of a small number of that original group to be invited to continue playing with this inspiring bunch of musicians. When I get the call to join their monumental adventure to Central Asia, I jump at the chance.

The group is made up of around fifty people, split between Western and Eastern musicians, staff, security, and a documentary crew. Those of us living in New York City (or close enough to travel there) meet several weeks before the tour to go over security protocols. We convene in a skyscraper in Midtown, where we receive our music assignments and meet with the security team, which includes a body double for Yo-Yo who is a martial arts expert. His main job is to carry Yo-Yo's cello, walking towards the front of the group to draw attention away from Yo-Yo, who will embed himself in the midst of the rest of the entourage. There are two other bodyguards, very large guys who look like Marvel characters, with thick necks and arms straining against the fabric of their shirts, while the head of security is more sleek and slender. There is also an advance team that will scout and secure each location several days before we are to arrive.

We are told to pack light, wear old but respectable clothes in muted colors, with no words on them. No cell phones, baseball caps, or style choices that will make us stand out more than we naturally will, which will be a whole lot. Stay together, talk softly, don't leave the hotels without prior clearance, and always be accompanied by a guard. It becomes clear that we are going to a part of the world where we might be seen as targets for kidnapping or worse. We go over the entire itinerary and are sent home with a rather thick packet of rules and potential dangers, which we review and sign.

Our first stop on the tour is Bishkek, Kyrgyzstan. After two days of travel, we land well past dark at a small airport and are ushered through security, which amounts to a woman in an official two-piece skirt suit carrying a clipboard, checking off our names from a list. While several men gather our suitcases, we are led by our security team to a line of black cars and minivans, some of which are bulletproof. We drive in pitch blackness, the emptiness of the steppes showing signs of habitation only where tree trunks to the sides of the road are marked with wide bands of white paint to guide the cars in an otherwise black night.

I am shocked to realize we have entered a city of more than a million residents, but with no streetlamps, stoplights, advertising, or light coming from shops or cafes. It is only the next morning, when I look out my hotel window, that my breath is taken away as I see the overwhelming splendor of the Ala-Too mountains, part of Central Asia's Tien Shan range. These "Celestial Mountains" tower over the city, a wall of jagged peaks covered in snow stretching as far as the eye can see in either direction, its tallest peak reaching over 24,000 feet. From the flat expanse of tan earth, which looks almost scorched, these peaks erupt, *violently*, like a frozen tsunami. My organized, comfortable life filled with tiny luxuries seems so far away.

This mountain range connects China, Kyrgyzstan, Kazakhstan, Tajikistan, and Uzbekistan, is 1,500 miles long, and, as a first impression of what I will be experiencing on this journey, it floors me. I feel entirely minuscule and unimportant, and at the same time, I realize that this is a pivotal moment in my life, one that will change the trajectory of both my career and my view of life itself. I grab my cherished violin and head out the door to start this next adventure.

Over the next days we rehearse and get to know one another. The small crew of Western instrumentalists is joined, among others, by an Indian tabla player, a kemanche virtuoso from Tehran, Iranian hammered dulcimer, Chinese zheng, and an Azerbaijan singer with his own backup band of traditional instrumentalists. I am one of only three female musicians, one of whom is a formidable Mongolian long song singer. When she sings, you can feel the power of her voice inside your own chest, and it fills every corner of the huge halls we are performing in. The strength and clarity comes from a long-ago era when these singers were used as a way of transferring important news across the steppes of Mongolia.

We play pieces that are a mash-up of old and new, just as our instruments and traditions are. Each rehearsal has several translators murmuring in the ears of the musicians who do not speak English. To communicate, people sing, gesture, demonstrate on their instruments, searching for a common language without words. Some pieces are for just a couple of people, some for the whole group, some straight classical music inspired by Asia, and some wild, evocative numbers with built-in improvisation sections, such as "Blue as the Turquoise Night of Neyshabur." A haze of curious-smelling smoke surrounds the rehearsals as members leave their pipes or huge, hand-rolled cones filled with fragrant leaves of some kind, with little squiggly sticks poking out, smoking in trays while we workshop pieces, swapping parts, adding new sections, changing notes and tempos. Yo-Yo is in every rehearsal, curiously asking questions of different musicians, learning new ways of playing his cello, and finding ways to commingle our sounds to create a new vision of what music can become.

The musicians sit together for meals, making jokes using sounds and gestures sprinkled with the few words we have in common. I learn a lot from these talks: how to listen to each other in different ways; how to allow a rehearsal to unfold slowly, naturally. Life lessons, too: how to pace and sustain a career in music; how to continually cultivate passion.

One Chinese musician I befriend grew up during the Cultural Revolution. Hong was a small child when Mao began what was to become one of the bloodiest eras in human history. The chaos that ensued mutilated the economy and destroyed millions of lives. He closed all schools and universities, and my friend's father lost his profession as a history teacher. His father was lucky that he survived at all, counting himself fortunate to be relocated to the countryside to work in the fields after spending years in prison enduring excruciating torture. Most of his colleagues died in captivity or were killed outright. Estimates of lives lost range from one to two million during that ten-year period and include government-endorsed massacres. Documented live burial, beheading, boiling, disemboweling and cannibalism. Music, both Western and traditional, was banned, and only revolutionary music was allowed.

In 1976 the cruel, senseless revolution died with Mao and traditional Chinese music was tentatively allowed again. Hong learned to play the pipa, an ancient Chinese lute, eventually becoming a big name in China. He is incredibly warm and energetic, with a huge sparkling grin, and we absolutely love playing together, tossing melodies back and forth or enjoying a shared tune in octaves. It's hard for me to understand how he can be so filled with joy when his entire childhood was imbued with death, suppression, and day-to-day survival. Often speaking in poetic flourishes, he sprinkles small nuggets of advice here and there. Determination overrides difficulty, fortune doesn't come twice, and a smile will give you ten years of life.

We chat about the exhaustion that comes with making a living by piecing together many different kinds of work. Hong takes my hand and tells me a story that has guided my life since that time. A lion crouches, quietly and patiently waiting to find the best prey. He stoically manages his hunger, saving his energy and strength. He does not run, chasing animals, wasting his life on meaningless tasks. And when he does locate his goal, he thinks, he plans, and with all of his stored energy, he pounces, devouring his target.

Hong says this is what a life in music must be. Do not use your important core strength on meaningless, everyday tasks that deplete your being. It is better to be hungry and to wait for the best opportunity. Use everything you have to tackle important prospects, sinking in with your teeth.

Several days into the tour, I introduce something called "*Fanny's Gonna Get Ya*." This highly intellectual game consists of me pointing to someone, calling out the words "Fanny's Gonna Get Ya," then chasing the person around, running backwards as fast as I possibly can until I catch them with my bum, at which point I grind them against the wall backwards until we collapse in hilarious laughter. I am pretty sure people like when I "catch" them, or maybe I am just the world's fastest backwards runner. It turns out this is a fantastic way to spend our bored time together backstage or in hotels, is suitable for any age or gender, and even members of the security detail and documentary crew sometimes get suckered into a round between doing their jobs or showing me some great new way to flip an opponent.

I am not the kind of person to have framed degrees on my studio wall at home or at my office; instead, I have things like memorable tour posters, embroidered portraits of my deceased pets, drawings of my favorite composers. But I do have a framed photo of Yo-Yo and me. Without telling me, my parents printed it and waited for Yo-Yo after a concert in Chicago, asking him to sign it. In the photo we are in a hotel in Central Asia. It's the last night of our tour, and I have my head back, eyes closed, and am laughing so hard you can see my tonsils. Yo-Yo and I are clutching each other with both hands; you can see our fingers indenting one another's bodies; his head is pressed against my neck, a huge grin on his face. Underneath, his writing says, "This is a post 'Fanny's Gonna Get Ya' shot. You're the best! XOXO Yo-Yo." When a friend of mine goes to see Yo-Yo, I tell them to try saying "Fanny's Gonna Get Ya" to him. And lo and behold, the texts I receive after the concert confirmed that Yo-Yo also remembers those days as he chases my friends around backwards.

The morning after the first concert we are driven to an airstrip with a private plane, which will be our personal transport for the rest of this journey. Walking up the stairs, I enter what I can only describe as a set for an old espionage movie. White shag carpets line the entire airplane, huge white leather couches face one another, bolted to the floor, with seat belts coming up through the cushions. There are also large regular airplane seats, but they, like everything else, look like they have been plucked from the overflow props department of a has-been Hollywood studio. We all settle in, and our perfectly manicured airline hostesses offer us small glasses of vodka and individual sticks of Doublemint gum from round metal trays. These women are expertly made up, with cravats, pencil skirts, nylons, high heels, and precisely creased small woolen hats perched upon their styled hair.

Landing on a private airstrip, I can see from my window a line of people waiting for us, with a red carpet laid out. As we exit the airplane we are greeted by a group dressed in traditional attire: long robes of vibrant single colors with thick stripes of white embroidery, heads covered by scarves or tall black and white hats with tassels. A group of musicians entertains us on bowed guitar-like instruments, lutes, and large round drums. The first person to greet us is holding a platter draped in an embroidered cloth with a large, round bread on top. I rip off a piece, dip it into the bowl of rough salt held by the next person in line, and after eating it, I nod slightly to each person.

We are treated in this sincere, profound way for the entire trip. Sharing ancient traditions includes eating foods such as horse meat, spicy noodle dishes, dumplings filled with meat and potatoes, and a tangy, thick, fermented horse milk drink. I decide to forgo my vegetarianism for this trip so as not to insult our hosts, and my taste buds are alive with new textures and complicated spices.

At night, as I try to sleep, fitful with energy from the day, I hear Yo-Yo practicing in his room, slowly and methodically, for hours, drilling sections and working on minute details. He works harder and longer than anyone in the group, all the while having meetings, interviews, and joining the musicians for meals. The security team is busy checking the performance venue, installing lightbulbs in the concert hall. I am told that we are traveling with our own large case of lightbulbs, which will be painstakingly installed at each venue, then removed to travel with us to the next location.

In every city, we are given private concerts and demonstrations of local music, history, and art. On one occasion, we are led into a large, empty ballroom which has, at the end, a small covered platform like a miniature amphitheater. Inside is an old, wizened man, with long scraggly hair, uncomfortably wearing a bright red sweater. It looks like someone dragged him out of a cave, put him in a shower, and pulled a brand-new sweater from Target over his head. He seems like a frightened wild animal.

They introduce this man as one of the finest epic storytellers in Central Asia, a person who had been called to this way of life as a child after having a prophetic dream. The selection of these great storytellers seems somewhat like the process of finding the next Dalai Lama to me. He actually does live in a cave and has spent his entire life dedicated to the task of memorizing and performing ancient legends of Central Asia. He has memorized the thousand-year-old *Manas* trilogy, an epic poem *sixteen times longer* than Homer's *Iliad* and *Odyssey*, which takes over one hundred hours to recite. This is the way the history of their culture was passed from generation to generation, traveling narrators reciting for illiterate, nomadic populations.

As we settle on the floor, he closes his eyes and begins to speak in a rhythmic, throaty whisper. Every several minutes he changes styles, going into loud chanting accompanied by slapping his hands in patterns on different parts of his legs and arms, then to a series of long tones, arms raised above his head. As a classical musician, I am accustomed to pieces with large sections ranging from fifteen to twenty minutes, but our man shows no indication of slowing down or stopping even after thirty minutes. This is a one-man show of heroic proportions. At several points he opens his eyes, and with a deep, loud shout, points to each of us in turn, staring straight through us like he is a human lightning bolt. I don't understand a thing he is saying, but I also know *exactly* what he is talking about. It is the same thing I am saying when I play Schubert or Brahms. The anger of an undeserved death, the tenderness of holding an infant, the sorrow of an unrequited love.

This level of dedication dwarfs any commitment I have ever encountered. The stories of being locked in a room as a child to practice for seven hours a day like Paganini are nothing. At least Paganini had food and a bed. A life of living in a cave, spending every waking hour memorizing and reciting the history of your people, the weight of being a chosen person. It makes even Olympic athletes look like couch potatoes.

After what must be forty-five minutes I settle in for the long haul. No longer wondering when this is going to end, I relinquish myself into something that resembles a trance. I soak up the vibrancy and kinetic energy, the otherworldliness, of this trip, of the people I have begun to know, the taste and sound of culture thick with devastating torment, courage, and ecstatic euphoria.

The rest of the tour is as surprising and fulfilling as it has been from the first minute, and as we check in at the final hotel, I am sad that it is going to end. We will all fly to Germany from Dushanbe, Tajikistan, the next morning, then split apart to catch the next flights to our various destinations.

But something feels different that night; the security team is tight, speaking in hushed, nervous tones. They keep us all together, making sure that everyone is accounted for over and over again. The advance team stations themselves by all the exits, and the musicians stay quiet and serious. It is only the next day in Germany, as we are saying our goodbyes, that one of the security team mentions that there had been an incident the night before. Someone had checked into the hotel, paid in cash, and had asked to be put in a room close to Yo-Yo. They had no luggage, just a backpack. The staff did not comply with the room request, but the person *did* stay in the hotel. Thankfully, it didn't turn into a dangerous situation, thanks to the diligence and coordination of our caring and well-trained security detail.

Instead of heading back home to Connecticut, I travel straight to Washington, D.C. I am giving my solo debut in two days at the Kennedy Center, playing the magnificent and supremely difficult Bach *Chaconne* for solo violin—violinists' own form of epic poetry. I learned many things during my trip to Central Asia, but the lesson I return to again and again is not to waste any of my life doing something that doesn't fulfill me. It's better to eat rice and beans with a clear head and heart than a steak with no soul.

7 Lost

A line of red welts is forming along the lengths of my taut, muscular arms. A bigger bulge, rimmed in purple along the outside of my thigh. Painful to the touch. I notice them just minutes before the concert, seemingly forming as I look in the mirror of my dressing room. White couch, Steinway piano, espresso station, tray with fruits, cheeses, and olives artfully displayed. I've had a rough day. Rough week, actually. No, make that a rough four months. Still out of breath, I have just barely made it to the concert, rushing from the police station, where I'd reported my precious violin stolen. Now, with minutes to go before curtain, a packed hall, and no violin to perform on, four professional violinists have arrived to generously offer a complete stranger the use of their prized antique instruments for the evening's concert. And yet I relish the challenge. There is a thrill in beating a series of obstacles with optimism and courage, and even as I am exhausted and heartsick over my own instrument, I am vibrating with the opportunity to succeed at something that seems surreally impossible.

A handwritten dinner invitation, in German, is propped on the makeup table under a wall of mirrors framed by bulbous circular lightbulbs. I am in Freiburg, Germany.

I am wearing a floor-length, eggplant-colored evening gown covered in swirls of sequins. It's an asymmetrical, body-hugging dress with a cutout at the middle of my back, but with enough shoulder coverage to hide my tattoo, a hieroglyph that says "embrace life," with arms encircling the symbols of an ankh (infinity), water, and a placenta. The cellist of the quartet has asked me not to reveal my tattoo to our formal, German audience, as it doesn't match our image. We are a serious, high-class string quartet. A Mercedes, not a Buick. My hair, as usual, is a three-dimensional expression of my personality. Saucy, bouncy, hard to control, and with a mind of its own. People often remark on it, how it seems to mirror my moods, maybe even anticipating my next dramatic flourish during concerts. I always wear flats, not only because I am six feet tall (the same height as the rest of the members of my quartet), but also because I will be performing standing and will need a solid foundation from which to pivot to the audience, execute precise directives, and perform like a violin virtuoso as is expected and demanded, by myself as much as my colleagues and audience.

I have continued to lose weight these past four months, since moving from Corvallis, Oregon, to Berlin on three weeks' notice to join the Artemis String Quartet. It's actually been fun to have to go shopping for new clothes in smaller sizes. I quickly realize that my Oregonian fashion sticks out like a sore thumb in the rather staid and monotone Germany. An evergreen vintage knee-length leather skirt and a button-down shirt with teeny stitched mushrooms on it? *No. Not fitting in.* I like to think I am looking more European now, with my new black, gray, and tan clothes, but who am I kidding? In every review, newspaper article, and radio show they treat me like some kind of exotic species, commenting on my loud laugh and funny accent, even the way I energetically walk on stage. And this is while I am doing all I can to suppress my boisterous personality.

I'd stopped stepping on the scale a month earlier. I don't have time or brain space to worry or think about that. It's not that I am not eating. I am. And well, with lavish, multicourse post-concert meals around elegant tables well into the night, with aperitif, beer, wine, and digestif woven through the parade of dishes. *London, New York, Amsterdam, Berlin, Vienna, Chicago, Toronto.* More than thirty concerts so far. I am losing weight because I don't have a moment to recover in this hectic, tantalizing new world. A world of limos, managers, publicists, immense concert halls, interviews, and post-concert signing tables.

And in the meantime, I become a professor at the University of the Arts Berlin (the largest music school in Europe, dwarfing the Juilliard School in New York) as well as Master Teacher at the elite Queen Elizabeth school in Brussels. It's no wonder that I begin to lose things. I can see now that they start to slip away the moment I call Jason from Berlin in January of 2016 to tell him I have been invited to join the Artemis String Quartet.

When you lose something—your relationship, your home, your health, your way, your nerve—it can be hard to pinpoint when that actually begins or if it can ever end. Sometimes losing something means gaining something else. Sometimes you can't tell it's happened until years later.

When I accept the position, I naively think life can handle as much as I can put into it. Like life is an endlessly expandable balloon; you can keep adding and adding things, and it will *never* pop. And I push through, like I always do. I have the babies; I have the partner; I have the job that violinists lust after. I have never wanted to get married; I want to just have a family without the external pressure of marriage. With no legal document, there are no excuses to behave badly to your partner, no obligation to stay. It's only you and that other person, staying together because you want to. Because you *fight* for it.

Another thing that happens in those four months? You guessed it: I get married. I don't want to, obviously. But in Germany, they don't recognize domestic partnership, and Jason is going to be deported for being a single man with no job. They won't give him a visa. He is just some guy visiting Germany. And I am a single mother of two. So. We get married at the courthouse in Eugene, Oregon, and honestly, even though it is adorable and sweet and I wear a $23 wedding dress from the Goodwill that my daughters pick out (complete with a twenty-year-old lasagna stain on the front), I am not sure I am happy about the whole thing, even now. It feels like someone else is all up and in my personal business.

When I think back to those four months leading up to the theft of my beloved violin, my chest tightens. Because of the things that I love so dearly, that I almost lose during that time.

Some definitions of *Lost*:

Unable to be found or find your way, no longer possessed, very unhappy, so interested in something else that you do not notice other things, ruined or destroyed physically or morally, overlooked during a process or activity, self-absorbed.

Things I am in danger of losing during those first four months in Germany:

- My own life: I have my first life-threatening anaphylactic allergic reaction and two near misses with terrorist bombings.
- My health: I am losing weight, have a precancerous growth removed from my back, and am soon to be rushed to the hospital for emergency surgery.
- My family: I give up my role as lead parent, and tension with Jason is bringing our very relationship to a tipping point.
- My home: we've left our country, friends, and family with short notice; I feel like I am losing everything, from our house to all of the things inside it that don't fit into a suitcase.

But I am still clinging to my conviction. It isn't enough that I won this job. I am going to be everything they hoped for when they chose me. The best violinist, the smartest, most charming, loyal, and responsible quartet partner. I am going to provide life-changing experiences for my children and give Jason the platform to create his own career in Europe. No wonder I start to lose myself. Who can possibly fulfill all of these expectations? I can. *I swear I can.*

Before the Artemis Quartet goes on tour, we have a tradition of performing three "house concerts" in Berlin as a dry run, a chance to test the hard work put in and to tweak any details before hitting the road and performing for packed audiences in legendary concert halls. When I move to Berlin, I am already an experienced performer with more than a thousand performances under my belt, able to replicate almost impossible technical challenges without flaw in front of live audiences with passion and intense emotional commitment. But none of that prepares me for the depth and vigor of the Artemis rehearsals.

Looking back at our schedule, it's amazing I didn't get tendonitis from the number of hours I put in on my violin every day. The quartet is booked up to two years in advance, and our detailed rehearsal schedule is put together by our business-minded violist. It includes exactly which movement of which piece we will be practicing, for how long, and in which way we will practice (detailed intonation work, balance and pacing, structural work, recorded and analyzed playthroughs). *Talk about German efficiency.* I count up the hours we practice together before our first tour, and it is more than eighty. That doesn't include personal practice or house concerts, which easily double the amount. All this is done in the space of three weeks, while carrying a new professorship in a new country.

The first house concert is in a penthouse apartment in the swanky area of Charlottenburg, just off Kurfürstendamm, one of the most famous streets in Berlin. It's like the Champs-Élysées of Berlin, with ritzy bars and sumptuous designer stores. This penthouse apartment occupies an entire floor of a pre-war building, with wooden chevron parquet floors and floor-length windows on all four sides, facing the street and the interior courtyard. I am buzzed in, take the private elevator up, and am ushered into a stunningly white room lined with modern art, from sculpture to textiles and paintings, some with moving parts or light emitting from them. This is like no kind of house concert I have ever played before—

well beyond luxurious. There is seating for more than one hundred personally invited guests, and my quartet point out to me the star of a Berlin crime show, a news anchor, and more. After the concert, the catered food is tremendous. Made-to-order fresh pastas, seared meats, marinated vegetables, and, for dessert, crème bavarois. This is a French/Bavarian dessert, like a dense whipped cream, with fruit embedded in the bottom—kiwi, which I've never had before. It is so delicious that I have seconds. I begin to feel lightheaded and decide to quickly say my farewells for the evening and start to find my way home along the cold, rainy Berlin streets.

Using the app on my phone, I find a car share on the street, unlocking and starting the vehicle directly from my phone (one more new thing we've encountered in Germany). It's a twenty-five-minute drive back to our quirky loft apartment in a converted factory in Kreuzberg, the Turkish area of Berlin. I step on the gas as I start to feel seriously woozy, hoping to make it back before I get even worse. My vision becomes blurry and my stomach starts to complain. I call Jason (the girls have been in bed for hours already) saying something is seriously wrong, I may have eaten something that doesn't agree with me. By the time I get home, I have already vomited out of my car window at a red light, I can barely breathe, I am dizzy, and my vision has narrowed to a pinprick.

As soon as I stumble into the apartment, my entire body empties in the bathroom in a series of spastic lurches as a red rash spreads across my body and my temperature starts to plummet. Jason looks up the symptoms on his phone and says I am probably having a severe food allergy, and if I can't breathe, we have to get to a hospital. I am lying on the floor of the bathroom, wheezing, my face swelling, unable to get up or speak.

I drink a whole bottle of children's allergy medicine as Jason drapes warm cloths over my neck and forehead, desperately trying to figure out where a hospital is, what the 911 number is in Berlin, how we can even find a cab or anything to get to the hospital in this industrial area at two in the morning, how we can make it out the door together with two sleeping children.

We can't find the right information; we are both utterly panicking and we simply don't yet have the skills to figure it out in a different language, a completely different set of rules and customs. Just at the moment when I think I may possibly die and it is too late to do anything, it stops getting worse. It stays the same, just for ten seconds. And we decide to ride it out. It all begins to fade, my body slows its jerking, and the vomiting and diarrhea decelerate. For the rest of the night, I stay on a blanket on the bathroom floor, in and out of exhausted drowsiness, as Jason checks on me every thirty minutes.

Right at this very second, I am curled up on a couch in the living room of our home in Oregon. Jason just came into the room, warm mug of tea in his hand, and I read this paragraph to him. We look at each other, reliving that frenzied night, realizing I could have died right at that moment. I *really* could have. And he would have been alone in Berlin, with a dead wife and two small children. *What then?* He says, "My God, people will read this and think we are total idiots!" But no, we did the best we could as overwhelmed and stressed parents, in a relationship that was uncoiling. As we held our breaths, we both noticed a distinct turning point, and as we always do, we made it through the storm together.

Things in Berlin begin to feel slightly more normal. I can now find mustard at the grocery store, we are looking for a permanent apartment, and Jason has played his first week as a guest in an amazing Berlin orchestra. The quartet has an incredible whirlwind tour to North America from Carnegie Hall to the Herbst Theatre in San Francisco with rave reviews. And yet another European tour. I am seeing Jason and the girls less and less, becoming a visitor in my own home.

I miss the Brussels Airport bombing of March 22, 2016, by a mere twenty-two minutes. It is a coordinated attack by the Islamic State. One suicide bomber detonates luggage carts loaded with explosives on one side of the main hall of the airport, and when survivors run in a panic in the other direction to escape the danger, his partner detonates a second cart on the opposite end of the space, catching people as they run. It is brutal, deadly, and psychologically impossible to process. The concert is rescheduled, and we carry on with our tour as planned. As shocking as this attack is, particularly with how narrowly we miss it, the bigger shock comes from the reactions of my colleagues and management team. They are, of course, horrified and deeply disturbed, but they are also somehow used to it and pick up and move on as if their strides were merely slowed for a moment. I begin to realize that terrorism, in its many forms, is quite common here in Germany, in Europe. The debris is cleared, the bombing investigated, and we tune our instruments and keep going.

Nine weeks after the Brussels Airport bombing, we head to Istanbul. I have been to Istanbul before, when I was in my early twenties. My sisters and I decided to drive from Paris to Istanbul, camping along the way, and the magic and mystical splendor of that incredible city still takes the breath out of me. I have a brief list of things I want to sneak in before or after the show, including a visit to the Grand Bazaar and the Hagia Sophia mosque, eating some flavorful street food, and picking up some fun gifts for the family (antique necklaces, Turkish delight, and if I am lucky, a nice rug). But I get a last-minute call as I am heading out the front door in Berlin. All flights have been suspended because of a suspected Islamic State bombing in central Istanbul, killing twelve people and injuring fifty-one others. There have already been four terrorist attacks in Turkey this year, and things are escalating. Suicide bombers, cars filled with explosives and detonated, Americans and tourists killed alongside locals. There are to be six more terrorist attacks in Turkey that year alone, including the assassination of an ambassador in an art gallery. For me, it feels like every time I start to find flow or a bit of comfort in this new life, a tragic event occurs. I am exhausted from constantly picking myself up and dusting myself off, giving myself an adrenaline shot of optimism, pretending to my colleagues and family that nothing bothers me.

To say I get used to terrorism is a devastating statement. Numbed, *yes*. Accustomed to a constant low level of anxiety, *absolutely*. Even when just walking around our neighborhood. The Berlin Christmas Market attack happens just a couple of blocks from our apartment. Twelve dead and seventy injured as an Islamic terrorist deliberately drives a truck into a bustling Christmas Market. Jason and the girls and I were at that exact location the day before, happily eating *lebkuchen* and drinking warm mulled wine. It is a different feeling of dread than the one I have become depressingly and apathetically used to in our own American version of terrorism. The lone gunman, the unhinged and emotionally wounded man. In Europe it is a sharp, quick fear that I start to recognize in myself. The types of attacks are more grown-up, organized, global, and often occur in multiples. Spread out over time or simultaneous, they occur in locations that are a part of my daily job, in public gatherings or travel hubs. I have no choice but to incorporate one more layer of constant stress into my life. One that comes with an added helping of guilt, because isn't it me who selfishly craves this career, putting both myself and my family in harm's way? *Big sigh. Big guilt.*

The concert in Istanbul is canceled, and I come home to Berlin for a couple of days before resuming the tour. Our personal assistant buys train tickets for the next concert on the fast train from Berlin to Basel, the ICE 279.

I think of this type of train as more like an airplane than an Amtrak. The tickets are expensive; the people are well-dressed, often traveling for business. The train only makes a handful of stops, bypassing the small towns, reaching up to 300 kilometers an hour. You can't just hop on and buy a ticket. The seats are assigned; the bathrooms are pristine; the dining cars have actual tables and food. Not a place where you would think a violin would be stolen from the luggage rack above your head. But that's exactly what happens on June 14, 2016, almost four months to the day of my first rehearsals with the Artemis String Quartet.

I nod a greeting to my colleagues as we wait for our train on the platform at the Berlin Main Station, a massive glass structure with fourteen train platforms. More than one thousand trains stop here every day. It's like a huge mall plus travel hub, with thirty taxis lined up outside, restaurants, chocolate shops, butchers, grocery stores, bakeries, clothing stores, pharmacies. The ubiquitous Currywurst stands, with large sausages turning on a grill, each one placed in a bizarrely teeny bun and draped with hot red curry sauce, the French fries nestled next to the wurst inside the paper box, with a miniature wooden prong to eat them with. Even at the platforms themselves, you can find small bakeries, the fresh smell of oversized German pretzels with coarse salt on top, displayed for easy access on what look like dollhouse-sized wooden coat racks. Sandwiches with fresh mozzarella, croissants, lattes, all at reasonable prices.

The trains, as you would expect, run like clockwork, arriving and leaving exactly as scheduled. You can find your specific train car and seat either by looking at the permanently displayed diagrams on the platform or on your phone. There is a train conductor at each door, checking tickets and scanning QR codes.

Our secretary books a window seat for me, part of a four-seat arrangement with a slender table between the facing seats. My seat partner is an older, well-dressed gentleman with a button-down cardigan and trousers, and we exchange pleasantries. Equipped with electrical outlets, beverage holders, and an ample, reclining chair, this is my favorite kind of seat in which to spend the day. To see the concrete of Berlin slowly change into smaller towns in fits and starts, the countryside expanding, church spires rising above old villages. My eyes happily drink in that verdant landscape. These moments alone, on a train, bus, or plane, are sacred to me. It is my only quiet time.

I carefully put my violin up above my seat on the ICE 279 in its worn, inconspicuous case, as I have done hundreds of times before, nestling my backpack in front of it. I take down my book and iPad. I am looking forward to six and a half hours of catching up on sleep and studying my scores. I never have enough time to do all I have to do; any spare moment I have is spent hunched over my phone typing, arranging my teaching schedule, hiring sitters and cleaning help for Jason, scheduling activities for the girls, doing interviews, double-checking travel and hotel details, and entering the information into our shared family calendar. Jason and I don't have time to talk through the details of our lives, so we resort to texts and our shared calendar to stay organized. I also have a weekly writing deadline for my diary on *Slippedisc.com*, which by now has 20,000 readers. The snack trolley comes by at regular intervals, the uniformed attendant taking orders for espresso, sandwiches, and food from the restaurant menu, all to be delivered promptly

A couple of hundred kilometers later, just shy of 1:30 p.m., I go to the bathroom as the train stops in Mannheim. I nod to my seatmate, leaving my book and drink at my seat, tucking my iPad into my bag. When I return to my place minutes later, I instinctively reach above to check on my violin. A cold wave speeds through my body as my hand feels nothing. No violin. Just my backpack and the various other suitcases and bags belonging to the people around me. I calmly ask my seatmate if he has seen anyone take my violin. My German, by this point, is faltering, riddled with errors, sprinkled with English, but understandable.

He says,

"Why yes, a young man comes. He takes it with no hesitation."

"What does he look like?"

"He must be a friend of yours, tall, young, very sturdy, walking quickly towards the front of the train."

I grab my backpack and head forward in the train, crossing my fingers that the "young man" he describes is somehow our bald, fifty-year-old cellist, playing a practical joke on me, the novice quartet member.

Moving as fast as possible, I race up the train cars, finding my cellist first. Ecki is tall, thin, bald, athletic, with electric blue eyes. The son of a diplomat, he was raised moving from one exotic post to another, finally settling in the wealthy city of Bonn, Germany (the birthplace of Beethoven), in the West. He is cool under pressure and excellent with people. No, he hasn't taken the violin. We have twenty-four minutes until the next stop in Karlsruhe, and every second is going to count. As I push forward to find my violist, Ecki alerts the train authorities, then heads back to my chair to gather information for the police.

The train is hurtling onward at top speed. Twenty-four minutes to find that man and my violin. I spot our violist next in the dining car, a large man with flowing brown hair and a generous beard. Gregor is from the south of Germany, from a family of musicians, and takes care of the finances for the quartet. More gregarious than refined, he is whip-smart and surprisingly quick on his feet. As I surge forward to find our first violinist, Gregor methodically searches every bathroom for a hidden violin. I continue to look through the luggage racks, ever more frantically as the next station approaches. I find Vineta, our first violinist, a gorgeous, tall, slender Latvian woman with an ice-white pixie cut, and she immediately goes to work on two fronts: social media and our managers and publicist. By that evening, her post online has reached past 100,000 views. Our managers begin contacting violinists in the region to search for a violin to borrow for this evening's concert.

I have time for one more sweep of the train, nervously feeling the seconds slip away. I look at every passenger to see if my case is tucked between or behind a seat. If I don't find my violin before the next stop, my chances at ever recovering it will be exponentially decreased. The thief must have known what he was stealing, waiting for me to leave my seat for just one minute, then smoothly and confidently taking my violin. He may head to a pawn shop or music store, but if he goes across the border to Italy or another country, my chances of getting it back are even slimmer. I send two important emails, one to my violin shop in Berlin, who sends an SOS to all violin makers and repair shops in Germany to watch for my violin, and a second to my readers on *Slippedisc.com*, which helps broaden the search greatly.

Barely suppressing my spiraling devastation, my hands become more desperate in their search. I have had that violin by my side for thirty years, and I have never had to worry about it. What would I do with no violin, and a concert that night and every day that week? How can I ever come to terms with losing that last piece of tangible memory of my grandfather, that gift that has been nestled below my chin since I was a teenager?

As I step off the train in Karlsruhe, I feel myself slipping farther and farther away. My arms yearn for my lost violin, my fingers moving as they remember every curve and corner of my instrument. I turn to see the train pull away from the station, my violin likely aboard in the hands of a stranger, to be callously handed over for cash, like some kind of back-alley drug deal. Vineta and Gregor remain on the train to Freiburg; Ecki and I have gotten off to file a report with the police. The police are organized and proficient, verging on kind at moments, even as they call me stupid and careless, a naïve foreigner. I fill out form after form, detached from myself, as if I am watching some kind of PBS police procedural on a grainy television. They have all the information for the investigation within one hour. We quickly jump on the next train and make it to the concert hall with minutes to spare. I put on my eggplant-colored dress, noticing the bruises forming on my arms from the frantic searching on the train.

I calmly leave my dressing room to choose a violin for the evening's concert and notice a message pop up on my phone from Jason. He can't handle it anymore. He is looking for a one-way ticket back to the United States. I don't have the time or energy to respond right now. I have to head to the stage, where the audience is eagerly awaiting the performance. I can only deal with one loss at a time.

※ 8
Found

My entire body tenses as I hear the officious footsteps approaching on the smooth marble floor of the Mannheim train station. I've taken the first train here from Freiburg this morning, intent on finding my violin. There is a German police officer behind me, as I expected. I most likely don't appear all that dangerous, seeing as I am armed only with a roll of tape and a stack of papers that read "*Gestohlene Geige.*" A photo of my violin and case, brief description of the time and location of the theft, a reward of €1,250, and some convenient tear-off tabs with a new email address, GeigeBerlin@yahoo.com. I already know it is illegal to be doing what I am doing. The front desk at the hotel told me as much, exceedingly early this morning, as they kindly printed fifty copies of my notice after correcting my first-grade German grammar. The violist in my quartet tells me (*did he just roll his eyes at me?*) that the police will not allow me to talk to them, but that is exactly what I am planning on doing. The police had taken my statement and sent the case to the Mannheim police station, they had my contact information for potential follow-up, and that was that. They certainly don't need a woman from Chicago to "help" them. That's not how it's done here. You can't just make a sign with tear-off tabs and tape it up, you can't hand it out, and you can't talk to the police. But as Napoleon once said, if you want something done, do it yourself.

The police officer is angrily clutching seven or eight of my homemade signs in his hand and is reaching for the one I had just taped up. Looking at him with bleary but determined eyes, I say, "*Bitte*," "Please":

"It is the violin my grandfather gave me when I was a child. It is my very life, my soul, and I feel like I have been ripped in two."

Or actually, I probably say something like, "Please, my female violin, my female grandfather gift, no sleep, I so sad, hurt on body, help, please, female violin."

Pausing for a sigh, he speaks in a firm, loud voice, for anyone to hear. A crowd of people is already gathering. He tells me (why is it that when a German tells me something, it sounds like they are shouting at me?) what he knows I know: that in Germany it is illegal to post things in public places. To display your contact information, to offer a reward. *All of it is illegal.* I meet his eyes, and we look at each other for a strong, silent moment. Then he says, "Follow me to the police station." Seriously? Am I about to get fined or arrested for simply trying to find my violin?

Never mind. I am already accomplishing part of what I had set out to do: get inside the police station. As we walk away, I am shocked to see that he left my notice hanging on the wall. Check and check, as far as I am concerned.

We walk through the huge train station with its beautifully arched entryway, large electronic boards displaying train schedules lining the inside wall. The somehow retro-looking square red words composed of small dots are updating constantly; the wall is like a gigantic Lite

Brite for adults. Flower sellers, coffeehouses, bookstores. I notice a large stairwell heading down, with a rich, meaty smell wafting up. Must be food vendors down there, also probably a subway line and more stores. I always love seeing the four-foot-tall rotating gyro meat funnel and the rotisserie chickens slowly turning on their spits, generously dripping juices onto a tray of cut potatoes below. I often pick one up from the U-Bahn station in Berlin as I head home from tour or rehearsal.

I follow the police officer as he walks briskly towards the tracks, completely ignoring me. He takes a sharp turn and leads me down the entire expanse of the station. Stopping in front of an unassuming door, he holds his card to be buzzed in. Inside the small vestibule, another buzz as the attendant lets us through to the waiting room. In institutional off-white, the room resembles a black-and-white movie scene of the front desk of an old psychiatric hospital: sterile, with a large L-shaped desk blocking entrance from civilians, the wall behind the counter lined with small shelves, a long wooden bench for waiting against the side wall, and an extremely scary woman in full police uniform standing behind the counter. *My* police officer, with not another word, continues through the room and walks through a door to the inner sanctum. Not sure what to do, I approach the woman, who has small beady eyes, the physique of a lumberjack, and the aura of a loaf of stale bread. *Wonderful.* I say to her, "Please, the police officer brought me here to talk about my stolen violin. Should I wait for him or follow him into his office?"

Or probably actually, "Please, the female police bring me with, wait I female door go in?"

I haven't gotten the hang of gendered nouns yet and am going all in on default female. I mean, let's get real, women have gotten the short stick for a long time, historically—I'm just doing my bit to even things out a tad.

The front desk officer just looks at me with an aggressively tired expression, like I am some kind of slow-minded forest creature, and says, "You can wait there. He doesn't want to see you." So I sit. And sit. If practicing the violin teaches you anything in life, it's patience and perseverance, and I have that in spades. I can outwait, outstare, out-anything just about anyone. And I am here to stay. Looking at my phone, it is 7:30 a.m. I settle in.

The bench, if you want to call it that, is intentionally uncomfortable. It doesn't even have a back or sides. It is actually just a slab of wood, just slightly prettied up. I take out my book, and the front desk lady must know I mean business. I am reading David Foster Wallace's *Infinite Jest*, and I am just about halfway through (probably around page 600). Americans can be surprisingly stubborn. There is a German saying that goes something like: Germans are like a coconut, hard on the outside, but once cracked, soft inside. Americans are like a peach, soft and fuzzy on the outside, as hard as a pit on the inside.

My mind wanders to the evening before. Lots to unpack there, from the frenzied train search for my violin, the concert, the text from Jason. *Oh God, the text from Jason.* I knew he was stressed, unhappy, lonely, and frustrated. Of course he was. If we had been in the States, switching lead parenting roles in and of itself would be an enormous upheaval. But on top of that, a new country, new language (he is actually quite good at German, having taken it in college and passed his doctoral language exam), the abrupt loss of his university job, family, home. No friends. Two teeny girls who need his attention at all times. But in my mind, I am thinking, okay, here I am with a women's studies degree, and I know that if the genders were reversed, it would be "suck it up and put on a pretty face." Women have been giving up their lives, careers, moving at the drop of a hat for their husbands' jobs for centuries. And not complaining. They even give birth to the children along the way. The two men in my quartet have kids younger than ours, with stay-at-home wives who coddle them like nursemaids, packing lunches for them, doing their laundry. I wouldn't dream of asking Jason to do any of that. I hire house cleaners, babysitters, make big pots of stew before I leave home every tour. Yes, Jason is a *Hausmann*, but can't I have it all? I don't even ask for it all. *Just most.*

This line of reasoning isn't getting me anywhere fast. Well, it actually is. It is speeding me towards a divorce from a marriage that I didn't even want in the first place. Speeding as fast as that ICE 279. I need to reason through this. Figure out what I want, what I need, and how to make that happen. I start to make a list on my phone. What I need right now. What I need later, and what I want. Find out if I can have both what I want and need. The long term, and the short.

Jason and I have been together since we fell madly in love in our mid-twenties. Our relationship, in the intervening years, has morphed into a rich, complex partnership based on mutual respect, constant hilarity, and love of music and family. Jason is a terrific father. Better parent than I could ever be. He is the calm to my driven nature. He is steady, cautious to my impetuousness, a great musical partner, and impossible to fight with. Like, literally, I can pinpoint two fights we have had in our whole relationship, and one was right before we got married a couple of months ago. So yes, I both need and want Jason now and later. I need my kids all of the time. Every single moment. Non-negotiable.

What do I want from my life now and later? For now, from the quartet, I want to succeed on the big stage. For at least several years. I want to make a recording, one that will win a big international prize. A documentary would be nice. *Oh, and maybe write a book.* And I want to do cool stuff like play in the Berlin Philharmonic and sit as concertmaster of a legendary European orchestra, maybe even be featured in the *New York Times*. Yes. That would be perfect. Long term? Live somewhere I love, with at least one good bakery, and close to both mountains and water. Somewhere my whole family would like to be.

I text Jason.

"I am so sorry you are desperately unhappy. I love you. Can you do me a huge favor and just sit on this until I get back? I want to hear what you are thinking about and support whatever decision you make."

He writes back, "ok."

So I sit. And sit. And sit. Officers come and go. Not mine though. Every hour I try to re-engage with the front desk officer. Can she call back and ask if they can speak to me? Where is the bathroom? What's her favorite place to get female lunch in the station? Does she play an instrument? At noon she says I will have to leave; they are closing for lunch for an hour. I grab my backpack and say, "Okay, see you in an hour!" I catch a glimpse of her incredulous expression reflected on the glass of the door as I push forward.

That Buick Skylark from my early twenties—with the multicolored octopus lazily draped over the top and sides, the eyeball on the hood, and handprints all over it—pops into my head. That car also had this weird thing where if I stopped, it wouldn't restart. I had to get out, put it in neutral, and, with the door open, push it as fast as I could with my shoulder rammed against the door frame, jumping in to make a rolling start. This meant, of course, always having to try to find parking that was heading downhill, timing yellow and red lights perfectly so I would always be in motion (*people behind me loved that*), and having exact change for the millions of toll booths in the Midwest. I had to gauge the traffic in advance, starting my slowdown very early to compensate for the stop-and-go traffic ahead, babying the gas pedal to keep it alive. As the toll booth approached, I unrolled my window, leaning my body out as far as possible to give change to the attendant or start to lob the coins into the bucket while moving. Of course, as you can imagine, a lot of my left-handed shots didn't hit their mark, and so my yogurt container of money had to be *very* full. Anyone riding with me was obligated to help, trying to get a quarter in the basket from the back passenger seat or wherever.

Once I got enough coins in, timing the raising security bar was my final hurtle. Sometimes I'd just barely coast through, jumping out to keep the car in motion as the arm smacked into the trunk. On a cold Cleveland day, one of my more spectacular maneuvers caught the eye of a police car. Pulling me over was pretty easy. It was the pulling away again that would be interesting. The officer walked around to my window, and I mentioned I was late for a quartet rehearsal. He started to pull out his ticket pad, and I alluded to the fact that I was pretty broke, a fairly obvious statement from the state of my car, with the exhaust pipe held on with a coat hanger and the driver's side mirror attached with duct tape. Could he possibly entertain a warning instead of a ticket if I played "Danny Boy" for him? Scratching his chin, a smile creeping across his face, he said, "That sounds like it's worth it for the story alone." I pulled out my violin (*my* violin, the same one stolen on the ICE 279, the one I am trying to find) and played my best, heart-rending version of "Oh, Danny Boy." I may have imagined the moisture collecting around his eyes as he looked towards that flat, gray horizon, but it saved me a whopping ticket.

I think to myself, if I can crack the Cleveland police, there has to be a way of cracking these German police officers. They can't be an entirely different breed, can they?

I leave the police station, deciding to follow that tantalizing smell I noticed earlier. I wander down the stairs, getting a coffee and vegetarian döner kebab from the rotisserie place. With pieces of grilled halloumi (a firm, Middle Eastern grilling cheese), diced lettuce, veg, and fries wrapped in a warm pita, drizzled in spicy sauce, it hits the spot. And will wonders never cease—a Dunkin' Donuts! Right next door. What any good Chicagoan knows is that cops love donuts. And Irish tunes, obviously.

I get the deluxe box, twenty-four donuts, a nice mixed lot. I find my way back to the police station, go through the double buzzer doors, walk up to the scary hefty door lady, and put the box on the counter. She says, in a shrill voice, "We cannot accept gifts here. That is a bribe. We are the police!"

"But," I say, taking a donut, "I can't eat all of these female donuts! It's too many donuts for me. I will just leave them here until I leave and throw them away in the female garbage bin."

It is coming on seven hours of waiting, and I notice several police officers casually sliding donuts from the box. *Including my officer!* At 2:30, he comes out and says it will be OK if I tape up the rest of my posters, just for the day. Aha! I make the rounds and return at 3:30, taking my regular spot on the bench. At 4:30, my police officer comes out from the back rooms, bringing with him a much younger man, dressed in jeans and a polo. The polo guy says to me, in perfect English, "Hello, Ms. Kreston, would you like to come back and talk with us about your violin?" Oh yes, *most definitely yes*.

The inside of the police station is quite spacious. A large room with desks in groups of four, partitioned; halogen ceiling lamps; and around ten uniformed officers working. Talking on the phone, looking at computers, just like you would imagine. My polo officer brings me to a table, explaining that he is plainclothes police, and he had gone to one year of university in the United States, which he liked very much. We chat a bit, and he says he knows I have been there all day but doesn't know what exactly I am hoping for.

I explain that I think I might be able to help, because I know exactly how big the violin is; maybe if they have CCTV, I can identify the thief. He states the obvious. Civilians cannot see police video footage, which they do happen to have, from four different angles. Well, I say, how about I give you the exact dimension of the case and violin? Or more descriptions of the violin, which is made in Chicago, probably the only violin made in Chicago in the whole of Germany? We start there, measuring out the size both with and without the case. He leaves the desk for a moment, coming back with my original officer. They decide it will be okay if they just show me a couple of still shots of people leaving the train with oversized luggage to see if my violin could fit inside. They have identified seven possible suspects and isolated some still photos of them with their bags. I am able to rule out three immediately. Then something surprising. They guess it wouldn't hurt *to show me the entire videos of those four remaining suspects.*

Following them into a narrow room, I sit at a long, thin table lined with multiple screens. A young officer to my right is in charge of scrolling through the videos, following the quick, staccato German instructions from my police officer. We get into a nice flow, the polo officer translating for me when I want to see slow-motion or rewind, as they point and ask specific questions about the suspects. This is why I had come. Why my butt is numb from that hideous bench, why I am on page 734 of *Infinite Jest*, why it's important to take my future into my own hands. After looking at the videos, I thank them for speaking with me; I am grateful for their time and hard work. In the coming weeks, the polo police officer contacts me on several occasions to check on details and new leads. I have a nice selfie of us together, both sporting big grins, which gives me a spreading warmth in my chest when it pops up on my phone's photo memories.

Definitions for *Found, Find*:

To begin or create something that is meant to last for a long time (establish), to come upon something by chance, to locate, attain, or obtain by search or effort, to recover, to gain or regain the use of, to ascertain by study or calculation, to feel or perceive, to discover oneself.

Things I need to find:

- My home/life: After Jason's text, and everything else that has happened, I am reeling with the realization of how terrible things have gotten.

- My violin: I am determined to find it. There is no way I am going to give up.
- My health: It's spinning out of control and I have no idea how to rein it in.

I have an astonishing experience at the concert right after my violin is stolen. Just as I am in my darkest moment, standing backstage alone with no violin, with the prospect of my marriage falling apart, and under enormous pressure to not increase the stress of the situation for my colleagues, a knock comes at my door. The concert presenter quickly and seriously leads me to a room. Inside are four strangers of different ages and genders, the youngest a boy who looks to be a college student, the oldest an elderly man who sits hunched over in a chair, all silently observing me. Four violins and bows are laid out on a table. These precious and costly instruments, which mean every bit as much to their owners as my violin does to me, have been offered, no questions asked, to a complete stranger to perform on that evening. The owners have made extraordinary sacrifices to get here on short notice, canceling rehearsals and lessons, finding care for their children.

I have only a moment to play each instrument, testing them all in an identical way. A full three octave scale to see the timbre of all parts of the violin and check for evenness of tone. A very loud and aggressive passage from a modern piece on that evening's program, and a high and simple melody on the top strings. With not a moment to spare, I pick the instrument for that evening, one that responds to my hands quickly, has a warm, burnished tone, and has a firm personality of its own. Turning to the four owners, I thank them for their kindness and generosity.

How am I going to go out on stage without my own violin, a 1928 Carl Becker made in Chicago? As a teenager, I remember spending many a glorious weekend afternoon in the Becker shop in the working-class neighborhood of Belmont, Chicago. Walking up the wooden stairs to the raised first floor of the tall, thin house; ringing the bell. Hearing Carl Jr. coming down the creaky stairs from his second-floor workshop above the family residence. He welcomes me and guides me up. The waiting area is filled with antique upholstered furniture, windows with heavy velvet drapes pulled back, the beautiful side tables with cut-glass bowls filled with brightly colored wrapped candies. Carl is in his sixties at the time and always happy to see my violin, which he fondly remembers being made by his father when he was a young child. Carl Jr. always wears a clean, short-sleeved button-down shirt, with a large jeweler's magnifying visor hanging over his forehead.

His workshop, which is opened to the waiting area, looks like a mix of an alchemist's laboratory, furniture store, and miniature warehouse of instruments. Bubbling concoctions, the smell of resins, freshly cut wood, tools in containers and attached to pegboards, the floor covered in a thin layer of shavings, and rows of instruments hanging high up on the walls, like soldiers patiently waiting for a command. At his long wooden worktable, he pulls his work light over and looks closely at my violin, turning it this way and that. He lowers his magnifying visor, creating huge hilarious eyeballs, making me giggle as he peers inside the violin. He points to a little mark here or there, asks how that happened (ran into my stand, hit the side with a magnificently huge up-bow motion), cautions me to be careful with this instrument. He then takes an hour or two to fix any blemish, smoothing the ebony fingerboard which has developed ridges from my fingers being placed in the same location thousands and thousands of times.

Then my favorite part. The sound adjustment. He asks me to play something, then takes the violin from me, putting a long silver tool inside to adjust the sound post, a cylindrical piece of wood the width of a pencil that stands vertically inside the violin under the bridge, held there by tension alone. A little tap tap here, and the sound of the violin is completely changed, opening, warming, or sharpening. He asks what repertoire I am playing and adjusts the violin to suit the particular demands of that piece. The Gypsy violin concerto "Tzigane" by the French Impressionist composer Ravel? More power up on the highest registers of the lowest string, please. The Bach *Chaconne*, a baroque tour de force that demands utter clarity? Clean tones in the first position are in order.

It's only later I realize how important the Becker family is to the entire trade of violin makers and repairers in the United States. Five generations of Beckers, from the mid-1800s to today, have been making and repairing violins, training luthiers, responsible for the foundations of stringed instrument making in North America. Having moved from Germany, they survived the Great Chicago Fire of 1871, rescuing the most valuable instruments in grain sacks and carrying them over the Chicago River.

My violin has been by my side my whole adult life, truly my sidekick, spending more time with me than any living creature. It has my voice, my Chicago accent, and has stood the test of time, holding its ground in concerts and competitions against many a mightier and loftier instrument. It has a warm, powerful dark bottom and a top sound that can cut through anything, soaring over a hundred-piece orchestra when I play concertos, whispering as I play a lullaby to my newborn daughter. It is tender and bold, quirky and reliable. It is me.

I can feel the ghost of my violin under my fingers as I grasp this unknown instrument under my arm in Freiburg, Germany. We have to get to know each other quickly, she and I. As we head out to the stage, my colleagues look at one another and share a moment of resolve. The new violin is shaky to start, but we gain confidence together. I am going to have to adjust on the fly, choosing different fingerings or bowings to compensate for the change of violin and its unique voice. I decide to enjoy the experience, to allow my mind and body to find their way, not thinking too much, but rather trusting and forgiving. After the first piece, we are backstage retuning, and the rest of the quartet give me a thumbs-up, a pat on the shoulder. *All is well.*

The next piece is Beethoven, for me the most demanding of composers. He requires the utmost in concentration and perfection; this is no time to let my mind wander. The opening solo in the second movement of his op. 59 #1 is one of those places that seem so simple, so easy in the practice room. Just four measures, pianissimo, first position. The delicacy reveals any weakness in technique, and to make matters more stressful, each member of the quartet plays the same melody, one after another, so comparison is quick and obvious. I had tried this solo out backstage, and it came out mangled and incoherent, but now it is smooth and in control. Vineta gives me a quick supportive look after I finish. Then, the solo note at the beginning of the devastatingly poignant slow movement. A single C, softly played alone by me before the rest of the quartet enters, a feeling of suspension, desolation, timelessness and yet urgency, a sound that is both hollow and the birth of a poignant sadness. These are my personal goals for this moment. I close my eyes and the sound comes out, different from my Becker violin, but with the same feelings and intentions.

As I am playing the concert, many things are rushing through my head. This loss, in many ways, sums up my experiences since moving here in early February. Let go, be open, be yourself no matter the circumstances. My voice exists independent of any physical thing. I am the same musician if I have an injury, lose my ability to play, am in a coma. It is inside. By the time I am partway through the Shostakovich, I can hear myself in the new violin, coming out gradually. This is what I have now. I left my life and possessions, brought my family, and my violin is simply the last of a list of things that I have lost. Or is it that I have found my sound? Myself? Maybe I have lost my violin and gained in internal resolve?

After the concert, I meet the owner of the instrument, a middle-aged female professional violinist. We hadn't had a moment to speak before the concert; I didn't even know what kind of violin I was playing. We talk as we walk to the CD signing area. It turns out to be an Amati, one of the most extraordinary violins in the world. From a family of makers from Cremona, Italy, active from 1538 to 1740, they are so rare that they are mostly kept in museums or private collections and are hardly ever played in public.

So, I had been playing an instrument that was over 300 years old and on gut strings for the first time in my life. Legend says that gut strings were first used by the god Apollo when he saw a tortoise and had the inspiration to make the first lyre, using the intestines from that unwilling donor to make the strings themselves. Certainly, they have been used for at least two thousand years, as proven by the recent discovery of a harp with still playable gut strings in a tomb in Thebes. Now made from the small intestines of sheep and cattle, they give a glow to the sound, and in the hugely popular baroque orchestras of Europe, they are used exclusively. The drawback? Quiet, and unreliable for intonation.

I did notice that I had to adjust my intonation *a lot* in the concert. After the first several minutes, I could not even play open strings anymore and used my fingers to dampen the strings and adjust as I went. As a second violinist, my duty is often to supply the middle of chords on double stops. My fifths required minuscule acrobatics during this concert and, not wanting to take the time to re-tune on stage, I made the adjustments manually, changing finger pressure and placement to create the perfect pitches. The owner of the violin says, "Well, that is certainly the first time something as modern and aggressive has been played on this violin. As a baroque violinist, I didn't know it was even possible!"

I am glad, in retrospect, that I didn't know what I was playing. Better to just trust your instincts and jump in.

The concert has been a big success, and I am filled with warmth by the caring and concern of strangers as well as my quartet colleagues. I am actually starting to feel a little bit better about the whole thing by the next afternoon, as I leave the Mannheim police station to catch the fast train back home to Berlin. I optimistically think I might even make it home before one a.m. I have done everything I can to find my violin. The next weeks will be crucial, and I feel much better knowing that I have a direct line of communication with the officers overseeing my case. I have a couple of days at home now, where I can be present and try to untangle the tight, messy knot that my new life has created. And I am encouraged by the German coconut that has opened to me on numerous occasions in the past twenty-four hours. The generosity of both friends and strangers is shocking and gives me hope for a future here in Germany.

And an amazing thing does happen. By the time I get home to Berlin that night, a donor has come forward. I have, on indefinite loan, a beautiful Italian violin from the 1700s and a gorgeous bow. It happens. I don't know how, but it does.

※ 9
Off the Page

I am in my early twenties, living in Cleveland. I'd graduated from the Curtis Institute of Music a couple of years earlier, then lived on a commune in Oregon and had a stint in Oberlin, Ohio. My childhood best friend, Imogene, has dropped out of college, and we live together in a decent place, up the hill from Little Italy and just a couple of blocks from a fantastic cemetery, where a person recovering from a major hangover can bring a peanut butter and jelly sandwich, a book, lay out a blanket, and enjoy hours of uninterrupted me-time. It's 1994.

I am, in retrospect, in the midst of a three-year break from my stressful, fulfilling, and self-critical life in classical music. This pause is a major turning point in my life, something that recalibrates me. It gives me the freedom to realize I'm not trapped in the life I had trained for. I have many skills, many joys and interests, and I learn how to make a living not based solely on my classical chops; I can be something and somebody else. My family is vocally perplexed and disappointed in me during these years, wondering why I am throwing it all away. The thousands of hours of sweat and dedication, the accolades and triumphs. I am learning that happiness and success are two unrelated things and often do not happen simultaneously. These years of self-discovery are possibly the most important of my whole life.

Imogene and I have a cool railroad apartment in a somewhat decrepit four-story brick building. The grayish carpet in the main entrance and stairs is matted, stained with years of stories, and smells strongly of regret. Our place has a big, nonworking fireplace in the front room and enough space for our shared menagerie of Aphrodite (lovebird), Kartoffel (dwarf Russian hamster), Gorgonzola (iguana), Chester (rabbit), and Frank (degu—a kind of miniature Chilean kangaroo). We both fiercely believe in independence and freedom for all living creatures, so they are more often than not found flying or scampering around the apartment. We usually have several of the animals with us on our outings to the cemetery, with small, handmade vests and leashes we sew or crochet to keep them warm and safe.

We eventually fall in with a ragtag group of people who also seem, *refreshingly*, to have no idea what they are doing with their lives. People you see again and again when you frequent the same cheap bar and deli or share a cold Cleveland sidewalk to grab a smoke. Satisfied by merely existing.

I am making a small and steady living subbing in orchestras around Ohio and find my way into a fairly satisfying and entertaining side gig of playing in the pit orchestra for traveling musicals (like *Miss Saigon* and *Les Mis*) and arena shows, such as Page and Plant and Pavarotti.

Imogene and I have been best friends since first grade, when her family moved from Washington, D.C., to Winnetka, Illinois. We were in a lot of the same classes as kids, including Ms. Cole's, who had a large aviary in her fourth-grade classroom. We all had to take turns coming in early to clean the cage and feed the birds, and when it was Imogene's turn, she would sometimes absentmindedly leave the cage door open and we would spend several memorable hours catching finches flying around the long corridors at Greeley Elementary.

She has an erratic sense of humor that is beyond absurd and a long history of psychological problems, in and out of therapy since they first realized something was a bit unusual in sixth grade. She'd been pulled out of high school for suicidal behavior and diagnosed with a host of things. I can't remember what the final diagnosis is, but I've heard words such as depression, dyslexia, and schizophrenia mentioned. She can't keep it together in college and doesn't know where to go or what to do.

Her well-meaning parents often miss signs that she is declining, or her mother suggests oddball solutions involving types of food and herbal treatments. Her mental health is much rockier than they allow themselves to realize. I can't figure out why they don't take it more seriously, and there is not much I can do.

One day Imogene calls me from college. She is attending an elite liberal art school on the West Coast. I know she has been struggling, but I can hear something different in her voice that day. Her friends are starting to abandon her, sick of her ups and downs. She's talking in suicidal language, desperate and exhausted by her daily struggles to stay in college, to even get out of bed every day. She has dropped out of class after class, is on academic probation at school, afraid of what her parents will say.

"Imogene," I say, "pack your duffel bag and a couple of PBJs, throw them in the back of your car, and drive here right away. Don't think about it. Just do it."

And she does just that, barely stopping along the thirty-six-hour trip to Ohio.

For the next two years, I do my best to give her the help and support she needs to find her bearings. I stay on top of cooking, cleaning, shopping, and making sure bills are paid, and offer the basics someone needs to survive. But I'm not perfect. I have my own stuff to figure out.

Living together is as good as it can get. We understand each other. But I also know her illness is more than we can handle, just the two of us. We poke around Cleveland and find her a weekly therapist as well as a drop-in mental health facility where she can hang out, and I try to help her stay on her meds. We basically spend most of our time stoned, chilling out to music, wandering in the cemetery, reading, taking community classes in woodworking or whatever, and going to bars and parties. We cut each other's hair short, get some tattoos, and usually have a great time doing absolutely nothing. My hairstyle is close-shaved in the back with an unruly tuft at the top, which pokes up in irregular semi-dreadlock sausages. On non-workdays, I usually wear a pair of oversized army boots, a floor-length kilt, and old white t-shirts that I write messages on with a sharpie, stuff like "incongruous eggplant" or "surreptitious pancake."

One evening we find our way to a party in a part of the city we haven't been to before, following directions given to us by someone at the video store. Old Victorian houses covered in graffiti, with boarded-up windows, skinny streets, and no traffic lights. Little mom-and-pop stores and bars nestled amongst the houses. The whole neighborhood has the vibe of a funky Brigadoon. We've been told it's a costume party, so Imogene and I show up in single-colored bright polyester suits, pink lipstick, gobs of light blue eyeshadow, wide-brimmed, flower-festooned hats, and my grandfather's poker-chip caddy.

The house is packed to the brim with dancing bodies, heavy smoke, and loud music. We eventually head out back to get some air, hit the kegs, and hear the band. And there she is: Luna, singing lead in front of a feminist punk band. She is lithe, with the kind of thick, long black hair that looks like it's been taken right off a mannequin. She is gripping the mic, singing about an albatross or something, and I perk right up when I notice she has an electric violinist in her band. I catch up with her during a break and introduce myself.

"Hey, great band, do you write your own stuff?"

"Cool. Yeah."

"I love it that you have a violinist in your band, I also play violin."

"What kind of player are you?"

"All kinds."

Turns out her violinist is moving back to West Virginia, and they are auditioning new people. *Fantastic.*

We set up a meeting at the coffee place around the corner for the next afternoon to talk about me playing some gigs with the band. Luna is a florist during the day, in charge of installing and maintaining large plants in some of the downtown office buildings as well as supplying fresh-cut arrangements for the front desks. She's a single mom; her son plays bass guitar in the band and they look more like siblings than mom and son. She had gotten pregnant in high school and dropped out to have him. He is pretty cute, has her same dark hair, which falls halfway down his face, and wears punky leather pants and dark eye makeup. Their drummer is a pale, waif-like girl who fades into the background when she is offstage but has an on-stage persona that is borderline frightening, screaming stream of consciousness apocalyptic nonsense into her mic every once in a while during a lull. Luna writes all of the songs. They have a couple of albums out and a fairly busy schedule of gigs at disgusting bars and as opening acts for c-level bands.

Our rehearsals are at Luna's place, which is part of a semi-converted stables of an old estate just outside of Cleveland. The main house and all buildings have been made into apartments, but you can still clearly see that this was once a grand property with a large, white wooden colonial main house with two wings. Luna's part of the stables is a big space with high ceilings, a small kitchen along the side, and a bunch of old couches and stuffed chairs that look like they have been salvaged from the sidewalk on garbage day. It all has a decidedly funky, musty smell, a mix of a lot of cigarette and pot smoke and stale alcohol, and I swear I can smell ancient horse poop in there, too.

There are guitars, drums, trumpets, instruments of all kinds everywhere, hanging and propped. I unpack my violin and realize I have kind of blown my cover. I was bluffing my way here, but now it's as clear as day. I don't even have a pickup or amp.

"No worries," she says, "we can just play some of our songs and you can play along."

I just pretend to be really cool and relaxed, but what am I doing here? There isn't any music, not even a list of chords or anything. What does she mean, "play along"? I just nod with my eyes sort of half-closed and my heart racing and pretend I know what is going on. I probably make a complete fool of myself, but after an hour or so, she gives me some CDs and cassette tapes of songs to "learn" and we set up the next rehearsal.

Thus begins my year of playing with Luna, which is glorious and stupid and fun and memorable. Luna's son develops a crush on me, I buy a junk violin that I cover in stickers, learn how to use a foot pedal and effects processor, and how to "play along." Rehearsals start when at least two people have shown up. Luna writes some lyrics on the big chalkboard on the wall, her son starts to strum some chords, the drummer adds rhythm and spoken word, and I double Luna's melody or harmonize, sometimes taking a solo.

Luna starts to sing a tune she made up, which is always changing because no one knows how to read or write down music. But eventually it starts to take shape, and her lilting, mesmerizing voice finds and remembers the patterns that seem to just float out of her head. I offer to write down the tunes she sings, and the chord progressions her son is experimenting with, but there is no point, is there? I am the odd man out here, looking for structure and organization. I am the one who needs to learn, not the band.

A successful gig is measured by how much beer has been spilled, the fees are often counted out in crumpled dollar bills, we sometimes sleep in the car between gigs, and I learn how to go with the flow with my violin playing. All of those rules I learned in school? Don't matter here. No one even knows what a sixteenth note is.

When I am playing with Luna, late into the night, after countless beers and whatever else is floating around, I can't tell when the song is going to end or even remember what song we are on. My whole life has turned into one long run-on sentence, and when my A string breaks one night and I realize I don't have a spare, I finish the gig just playing on the three remaining strings. The next day, I drive down the hill and walk into the Cleveland Institute of Music, one of the best music schools in the country. I hear that there is an instrument supply store tucked into the basement of the main building, and I need to replace my string and get some more rosin.

As I meander around the huge modern building looking for the store, I hear someone call my name, "Sarah?" Hmmmm. Probably meant for someone else. I don't even bother to turn around. Then a quickening of steps and a tap on the shoulder. "Is it really you?" It's an old acquaintance, a very fine cellist from Chicago. We spent a summer together as teenagers as part of a highly selective summer quartet camp at Tanglewood. She says she barely recognizes me from behind, but who else is six feet tall with crazy auburn hair? We chat for a couple of minutes; she knows I had gone to Curtis but no one had heard anything about me for a couple of years. *I had disappeared.* She scribbles her number on a slip of paper and hands it to me. Her quartet is looking for a violist, has a spot at the Yale summer school in Norfolk, Connecticut, for the summer (all expenses paid) and would I be interested in joining them? I take the paper to be polite, but seriously, I have a sweet summer of crappy gigs with Luna lined up, and I am *so* over the classical scene. *So* yesterday.

The next week, we have a lot of Luna rehearsals, workshopping new songs for the next album and summer tours. Imogene and I decide we could use a bit of space and move deeper into Cleveland into two smaller apartments in the same complex. I have been admitted into Cleveland State University's First College program where I am going to start a Women's Studies degree in the fall. The last thing I need is an uptight classical string quartet going to Yale.

That week Luna's group has our first big fight. There is a song about a nasty breakup, and we are playing it in G major, making it sound pretty playful and happy for a depressing, angry song. I suggest trying it in the relative minor of E minor, and the guitarist says:

"But we're already playing it in E minor!"

Long story short, I can't convince them that we are actually in G major, even using the big chalkboard to demonstrate. I lose the argument, feeling like such a total idiot and loser. I have a degree from the best music school in the country and I don't even have my crap together enough to explain the difference between major and minor to these guys.

Things are starting to shift. My life begins to have focus again, I stop going to so many parties, and now that I am going back to school, I clean myself up a bit, sobering up and starting to think of what I might want to do with the next part of my life. I realize how much of my time and energy have been focused on Imogene and her day-to-day needs, and how I have been coping with it by numbing myself with drugs and alcohol. She is my best friend, but I can't manage to stop her from slipping away into her own world.

Imogene rarely goes outside these days. Since moving out of our shared apartment, she spends most of her time alone, not going to the mental health day facility anymore and having trouble with the basics. Food preparation, hygiene, sleep, reality. She's deteriorating, and I am increasingly concerned, but I don't have the time anymore to go over as much as I used to. My life is slowly starting to get back on track, as hers is quickly slipping away. Sometimes I skip my check-in visits days in a row.

One day I drop by, and she doesn't answer the door. I can see her Toyota parked in front, so I know she's home. I knock and bang, eventually with both fists, against her front door, calling out her name. Pleading with her to open. I phone her parents to see if they know anything. She eventually answers the door, slowly. The apartment is a mess: dirty, smelly clothes everywhere, not a scrap of floor to walk on without climbing over this or that, and disgusting dishes piled up on surfaces. Her easel has a painting of a woman, staring straight out, blood dripping from her eyes. I hug her, both of us standing and crying for what feels like forever. I realize I can't take care of her anymore. She is as close to the edge as I have ever seen her.

I know instantly that she needs more help than what *any* of us can offer. I feel completely overwhelmed and more afraid than I have ever felt in my life. We both need a path out of this impossible, dark maze.

I call her parents again, and they immediately drive the six hours from Chicago, arriving that evening. I help them pack Imogene in the car, and she is committed to a high-security mental institution in Chicago. I drive out the next weekend to see her, going through a metal detector to be admitted. They confiscate a plastic bag of crackers; it's a suicide risk somehow. Imogene and I sit together for our allotted thirty minutes, not knowing what to say as the guard looks on. The institution has the feel of a jail, with metal tables bolted to the floor, nurses in hospital attire, guards in gray outfits, and metal grates over the windows.

Imogene stays there for three weeks, then moves to a full-time mental institution in Massachusetts. She spends the next nine years of her life connected to that place, first as a full-time patient in the hospital, then in a group home, and finally in her own apartments as an outpatient. That institution has everything a person needs and caters to the wealthy and famous. James Taylor and Judy Garland spent time there, and Judy's specially installed matching lavender toilet and sink is still in the cottage. Coincidentally, during her time there, Imogene is just down the street from Tanglewood, where I spend the summer with that very same cellist who found me in the basement of the Cleveland Institute of Music and where I would later meet and work with Yo-Yo.

It's a long, bumpy road ahead, but Imogene is nothing if not determined and creative. She finds a community, a beautiful town to live in, and with support, she forges her own path.

The day after I get back from seeing her in the awful, oppressive Chicago mental facility, I take out that crumpled piece of paper with the phone number on it, call the cellist, and thus start my path back towards classical music. I realize my days with Luna are over, and I need to start new. The quartet I join, the Avalon String Quartet, is my absolute passion for the next seven years of my life, and we slowly and diligently work our way up to become one of the top young quartets in the world, winning international competitions, finding management, touring extensively. It is through this quartet that I meet the Artemis String Quartet from Germany as students at Juilliard, and later my future husband, Jason, in the cafeteria in Aspen, Colorado. These chance meetings change the course of my life forever.

※ 10
Meetings

I've heard about them from a bunch of people. An amazing German quartet, about my age. They had already studied with the Emerson Quartet in Aspen, who raved to me about them. All of the top American and Canadian quartets already know each other from summer festivals and competitions in North America, but the bigger, *international* things are what my quartet is gearing up for. That's when we will meet quartets from Asia, Russia, Europe. In order to cross the pond, we have to have already proven ourselves in our own countries, achieved the highest point, had a career, a track record. Which is what Artemis has done by making it to Juilliard in New York City. They have risen to the top of string-quartet playing in Germany, probably the toughest market in the world. It's where Beethoven, Schumann, Brahms, and Bach are from, has the highest concentration of orchestras, the most concerts, the best audiences. They've done it, and I can't wait to meet them.

It's 1996; I am twenty-three, part of an American-Canadian-French quartet, the Avalon String Quartet. We are living in Cleveland, where we study with members of the Cleveland Quartet, but we are about to move to Illinois to work intensely for two years with the polished and elegant Vermeer String Quartet, an Israeli/German/American quartet with an active touring career. It's going to be our first official "job."

We will be the student quartet-in-residence at Northern Illinois University, which is a huge state school, ninety minutes west of Chicago, but it might as well be eight hours for all the isolation. NIU is all corn fields surrounding ugly concrete buildings. Being away from distractions has a lot of advantages for a young string quartet; we often practice six to eight hours a day in addition to hours of individual practice.

For quartets just starting out, chances to work one-on-one with a famous living quartet are rare. These opportunities are presented by universities that have a notable string quartet as faculty. After being selected by international audition, the student quartet is offered a two-year graduate residency, free degree of their choice at the university, weekly private and group lessons, their own concert series, a stipend to live on, and financial assistance to travel and enter competitions. It's a win-win situation: the young quartet has an apprenticeship with a veteran string quartet of global stature, and by winning competitions, the student group helps to publicize the university.

We are beginning to have some name recognition, having spent the summer at the Yale School of Music and working with the Mendelssohn Quartet at their winter festival. Playing some concerts that pay actual money and building our repertoire. We have a loose four-year plan, starting with competitions in the States, getting management, then moving on to international competitions once we have enough experience and financial support from individuals and institutions.

Around the same time, the Artemis Quartet wins a position with the Alban Berg Quartet. They will live in

Vienna, rather than in the Illinois cornfields. Similar, but oh so different. In the middle of one of the greatest musical cities of the world, home to Mozart, Schubert, and Haydn, the Artemis will be surrounded not by corn, but by culture and history.

They originally formed in Lübeck in 1989, and they are *way* ahead of us, having already won competitions and attended festivals not only in Europe but also the States. To have a career, you need as many high-profile people as possible to support you, writing recommendations, helping you to get concerts and management and recording contracts. The more you spread your wings, the more air you will have for liftoff.

I first encounter the Artemis at the Juilliard School of Music in New York City. They are part of an intensive quartet institute, as are we. Eight quartets have been selected by video audition, six of them from North America, one from Israel, and one from Germany. It's an all-expenses-paid week of lessons with the legendary Juilliard String Quartet: four musicians with deep knowledge, thousands of performances throughout the world, and a stack of much-heralded recordings. We are lucky to have the chance to work with their founder, Robert Mann, who has been first violinist of the Juilliard String Quartet for nearly a half-century and mentor to almost every active string quartet in the world. His sound, sensibilities, and deep understanding of the life of a quartet musician are invaluable to the young quartets who have come to New York City to work with him.

Juilliard is situated along Broadway and 65th street in the heart of Lincoln Center, housed in several behemoth buildings just a couple of blocks from Central Park. The first day of the workshop is abustle with activity. Arriving students sign in with the security guard behind an imposing desk, and as we receive our welcome packets, we realize that this will be a week we will never forget.

I am gregarious by nature and can throw myself into a group of strangers and be off to the bar that night, laughing and drinking and feeling like old friends before the break of dawn. *So it is for me and the Artemis members.* I first see them across the cafeteria at Juilliard: a group of three attractive, six-foot-tall German men and a short, rounded young woman with wavy brown hair, strong and stoic. In many ways, on stage the Artemis Quartet exemplifies their namesake, Artemis, the goddess of the hunt, with the first violinist as Artemis herself, leading her powerful, god-like acolytes into battle.

Entering that cafeteria, I see many old friends among the other seven quartets. The top level of the string-quartet world is very tightly connected. We meet again and again throughout our careers, in Jerusalem, Melbourne, London, and connect at festivals or competitions. Quartets further along in their careers show up as judges or mentors rather than participants or students, and the paths keep on crossing. I wave and call out a "hello" to the Artemis, intent on getting to know them. By the end of the week, I feel like we may have made a lifetime connection. We observe each other's quartets being taught in public master classes, share meals, and find an ease together that remains when we run into one another over the years. After the final concert, I go to a twenty-four-hour pool hall with some of the Artemis, and we drink well into the night.

They are preparing for two of the most prestigious international competitions, each held only every three or four years. Borciani in Italy and ARD in Germany, weeks-long competitions with multiple rounds, live audiences, and a panel of judges. They end up winning both, and these competitions launch them into a truly worldwide career.

Day after day, hour upon hour, the Juilliard Quartet picks apart every moment of the pieces. The Artemis plays Schubert's final string quartet, G Major, #15; a sprawling, magnificent work, so difficult that normally only older, well-seasoned quartets have the time and maturity to pull it off.

We are all here this week for the detailed work that we crave. To dissect something that has already been painstakingly put together, to re-examine every instant, both individually and collectively, to refine, retune, reconsider, and revise. To elevate the already mastered piece to a new place. Tear it down and rebuild it. And the Artemis show us what is possible. *What is impossible.*

On the final day of concerts, Artemis is the last group to play in the crowded concert hall. After nearly fifty minutes of listening to their Schubert, I feel like my insides have been torn out. Like if I don't live another minute, I have seen the beauty of life; have drunken deeply of its secrets. I am mesmerized, and as the hall explodes into applause, I reach up to find my cheeks wet with tears; tears of ecstatic joy and devastation mixed, that special recipe that only Schubert can create, which eludes many musicians, and which, that night, makes a stamp on my heart that I can almost physically feel.

Over the next twenty years, we meet here and there. We drink huge steins of beer late into the night at Oktoberfest in Munich, spend a glorious week together in Schloss Elmau in the Bavarian Alps, and even run into one another in an airport now and again, on our separate concert tours. I travel to hear them perform whenever possible.

By 2005, the Artemis String Quartet is one of the most

celebrated living quartets. They are sleek, gorgeous, super-powered. Known for their passion and intellectual precision, they are masters of their art. They play to superfans in sold-out crowds from New York to Tokyo, record with top labels, have a prestigious teaching position, and are showered with every conceivable international accolade. They get married, start families.

In 2015, there is tragic news. They are searching for a new member; their violist, Friedemann Weigle, has committed suicide. This is a visceral loss to the music world, like losing Kurt Cobain, Anthony Bourdain, Robin Williams. He was someone we all knew from recordings, had seen on stage. His warmth as a performer, his generosity as an educator, and his commitment to the art form inspired us, lifted us up, helped explain the unexplainable. And that spirit permeates everything the Artemis stands for.

It's October 2015, two months after the Artemis String Quartet announces that it will have auditions to find a fourth member. Having a public job opening for a quartet is highly unusual. Normally, replacements are handled quietly, behind closed doors. Private auditions, whispered recommendations. If the word gets out that a quartet is looking for a new member, presenters may cancel concerts and the audience gets nervous, wondering if the group will be forever changed, or able to navigate the difficult task of integrating a new partner.

I am on tour with my trio, and I bring up the topic casually, walking around a leafy college quad.

"Jason, what do you think? It seems impossible, but do you think they could be interested in me? Is it even something worth poking a stick at?"

Jason, my partner in every way for the past eighteen years.

I'm thinking that they have surely, by now, found someone already or have at least narrowed their search to a few select possibilities. And they have always, in their twenty-six years together, had a three-man, one-woman ratio. Continuity of appearance will certainly be on their minds; will they consider changing that ratio to half men, half women? Plus, an American? A non-European? *Pretty unlikely.* European quartets aren't like quartets from North America. They pride themselves in their national identities. A Polish quartet will have four Poles, a French quartet, four French musicians. In America things are all mixed, and genders are much more evenly represented. String quartets are still very much a man's profession in Europe. I would be the only American woman in a leading European quartet, the only American violinist. *Just not going to happen, no matter how good I am.*

I would have to be good enough to overcome not only being a woman but also not European. That's the kind of challenge I like, my kind of odds.

Not only is it improbable because of what the Artemis may be looking for, there's also the course my career has recently been on. Five years ago, our trio decided to go into semi-maternity leave to allow Jason and I to have our two daughters and raise them in a normal, small-town atmosphere. I've been off the fast track, with not a lot to show for myself musically in that time. Also, will the Artemis even remember me? And if so, will that count for or against me?

The most incredible thing to me, in this whole unbelievable story, is the unwavering belief that Jason has in me. It is strong, without reserve, calm and secure. While walking and walking around that quad, which we do for hours that fall day, talking about every possible ramification and detail, the only thing that Jason knows for certain is that if I begin this process, our family, with our adorable three- and five-year-old daughters, will be moving to Berlin. I think the possibility is one in a thousand. He knows it is one hundred percent.

What follows is a series of start-and-stop events. I write to Eckart, the cellist of the Artemis. I hear back three weeks later. His email contains things like:

"Where is Oregon? What are you doing now? Yes, I remember you."

Two weeks pass.

The next messages come closer together.

"I remember that you are strong, nice, and a memorable performer."

My percentage moves to one in five hundred.

Then, when I'm on a solo tour in Charleston, a request for a virtual meeting.

I am floored. *Totally floored.*

Eckart and I speak, remembering the handful of times we have met. We talk about Jason, who he has also met, and our family. Then:

"I encourage you to submit a formal application. We may consider you, although we are at the very end of our process already."

The first big obstacle. The application needs to be sent in immediately. They have two hundred and forty applications that have already been submitted, and I will be the last, applicant two hundred and forty one. I need to include live footage of me performing in a string group such as a quartet, quintet, or sextet. Not a trio with piano, which is the only group I currently belong to. I have not played in a quartet in fifteen years and won't even be home from tour for another two weeks. When can I even find time to record something, and what would I play? I can't record a quartet; it would take years of practice in order to be polished enough to submit something at this level. I suggest that I put something together specifically for them, a piece for viola and piano?

The cringe and sigh from Eckart on my iPad says it all. Back to one in one thousand.

The job posting is for *either* violin or viola, but won't I shine more as a violist? When I met the Artemis, I was the *violist* in the Avalon Quartet, not *violinist*. But Eckart tells me that their violinist, Gregor, also plays viola and is willing to switch if the fit is right.

Two weeks later, I book the concert hall at the university where I teach, ask a Russian pianist to play Brahms and Schubert viola sonatas with me, and hire a videographer. We have only two hours to record. I put on a gorgeous, chocolate-colored, satin floor-length dress. I add three old trio videos to the application, where I am playing violin. I can play both instruments with the same proficiency and I hope this versatility impresses them, and that the memory of me playing in the Avalon Quartet is strong enough to make up for my unconventional video.

I send it in.

Now it is December. I don't hear anything for three weeks, except for a cursory "Thank you for your application" email on December thirteenth. Jason and I don't mention it; of course it is the longest shot in the world.

Then, a request for another meeting, right before Christmas. And an emailed question. "Would you consider playing violin instead of viola?"

Are you kidding? I will play the flugelhorn with my nose if they ask!

My percentage has risen.

At the meeting they love the video, especially the violin portion. I should book a flight to be in Berlin in two weeks, staying for a week to have two rounds of auditions, and I must learn these eight quartets. Beethoven, *of course* (both middle and late periods); Dvorak; Shostakovich; Grieg; Mozart; Janacek; and Brahms. That's the equivalent of a *year's* worth of concert repertoire. I immediately book my roundtrip flight and hotel. I will arrive on January 7th, the day after my younger daughter's fourth birthday.

I am one of eight finalists. I now have a twelve-and-a-half percent chance.

For the next two weeks I am on lockdown. Every partition of every second is needed, organized. I cancel all work, and we move into Jason's mom's house in Eugene. I don't have time to cook or take care of the girls like I have been doing for the last five years.

Jason and his parents have to take over entirely. I ask for my meals in my basement practice room. I gulp and grab bites with my violin in hand, chewing as I drill difficult shifts, often with my three-year-old wrapped around my leg, tuning all of my notes according to their function in the chord. High minor thirds, low major thirds, louder root notes, lighter fifths. I pour over the scores to analyze and make decisions, studying recordings of my favorite string quartets. The Guarneri (oh, Arnold. . . .), Cleveland (such depth of character), Emerson (rock stars), Artemis (passion and precision).

I have to scramble to hunt down the sheet music and scores for these eight pieces, spending hours finding and copying what is available from the University of Oregon library, borrowing the rest from colleagues. I run out of paper at home and ask Jason to pick up more paper and hair conditioner at the store. He refuses.

"Why on earth would I get more paper? We'll be moving to Berlin in a month and that's the last thing we need, extra paper to give away! And a full bottle of conditioner? Ridiculous! Forget it. We need to start to pare everything down."

My God, the confidence.

So I end up printing the last movement on colored paper. Mustard yellow. It's the Grieg String Quartet, and it's one of three of the eight pieces that are completely new to me. Luckily, I know very well the viola parts for the other five, having studied, taught, and competed on them with the Avalon Quartet. So, learning the second violin part feels familiar, even with a different clef, different instrument and notes. My hair gets quite frizzy. Nothing I can do about that with no more conditioner.

I practice more than eight hours a day, spending the rest of my waking hours marking the score, studying. I work out several different fingerings and bowings for certain passages, so that I can be ready to adjust and pivot during the audition. I mark the structure of the pieces into my part: exposition, first and second theme, development, recapitulation, coda. The chord progressions. I feel the music inside of me; I am digesting the complexities of the emotions.

When I see a new piece of music, I am looking at dots on a page. Kind of like early prototype computer code. It's my job to decipher, internalize, and eventually own that code. I first, tentatively, engage with those dots. I take them off the page, pull them over my head, and wear them like a new shirt. After my practice session, I take that shirt off, putting those dots back onto the page. The next time I practice, the shirt goes on and begins to form to my body, becoming flexible and contouring to my desires and thoughts. I am surprised at dinner that night that I am still wearing my new shirt of dots, humming the music to myself as I do dishes. Every day, the shirt changes. I am tapping the rhythm on my leg while driving, dreaming the music, even practicing while I'm asleep. And soon, I can no longer distinguish the shirt of notes from my own body. These dots have melted into my blood, and I am one and the same with Brahms, Beethoven, Mozart. Hand in hand, heart in heart.

Each of the eight pieces has a completely different set of rules. The customs of the musical language of the time period, the specific composer and his compositional traits, what was happening at that point in his personal life, as well as politically in his region and country, in the world.

As a chamber musician, you are not only a highly trained technician, you are also a historian, a psychologist, a soothsayer. You must be absolutely perfect on your own part while knowing when to lead, when to follow, when to play *with*. How to match vibrato width and speed, to notice a delicate timing, to put your full force and passion into the group. To be one with it and at the same time, to change it, mold it.

I arrive in Berlin and take a taxi from the Tegel Airport to my hotel in the Mitte (middle) area of Berlin, former East Berlin. I will be here for a week, and I have booked a room that has a kitchen. I will be dealing with a nine-hour jet lag which will have me hungry at off times, sleeping at the wrong times. Eckart meets me that evening at a coffeehouse to welcome me and answer any questions I might have and go over the schedule for the next three days.

Because I have come from so far away, indeed the only applicant coming from North America, they have asked me to prepare both the first and second rounds simultaneously. The other seven finalists, who have completed their auditions already, had three weeks between round one and two in order to practice for the next round. But I have come with everything prepared. I am ready. Open-minded. *Optimistic.*

In fact, that's the one piece of advice Jason gives to me as I leave Oregon.

"Just don't crush them with your optimism!"

Ecki explains, over a cup of steaming chamomile tea and biscuits, that we will be doing the first round during the first two days. This will be four of the pieces, and we will play them, in entirety, with as little discussion as possible. To see if we find an instinctual, natural flow. Music without words.

We will eat lunch and dinner together as a quartet, to get to know one another. They are auditioning me not only as a violinist but also as a companion. String quartets have to travel together, present a unified front, be appropriately entertaining at post-concert events.

On day three, the quartet will meet to discuss and decide if I will be going on to the next round. If I do go to the second round, it will start the afternoon of the third day and consist of the remaining four pieces. We will work on these in detail, discussing, arguing our points, matching and experimenting. Deep work. Serious work. I will also go to the University of the Arts and observe a master class of their advanced students, of whom there are fifty in total. The students will be performing late Beethoven in preparation for a big competition, and Günter Pichler, the famous violinist of the Alban Berg Quartet, will be there. He is a former teacher and a mentor to the Artemis, one of the most important quartet musicians alive.

I know I will need stamina and clarity of mind to make it through. But I am so focused. So prepared. I try to sleep that night but I can't. Not really.

The next day I walk the twenty minutes along the

cold, gray, rainy boulevard to find our meeting space. It's in the Musikkindergarten Berlin, a free school for children age one to six years old. Childcare and education have little to no cost in Berlin, from six weeks all the way through college. In addition, every parent receives a €350-per-month, per-child stipend from the government, from birth to age eighteen, directly deposited into their bank account.

This particular *Kita* (kindergarten) was started by the world-renowned pianist and conductor Daniel Barenboim to educate the children of the musicians in his orchestra, the Staatsoper Unter den Linden, with more musical support from the musicians of the Staatskapelle Berlin. Musicians from these orchestras come in regularly to perform small concerts, teach lessons, and lead workshops. And of course Daniel Barenboim himself also comes to the school. The motto of the Musikkindergarten, written by Barenboim, is "Education through music, not music education."

Before coming here, I looked up the members of the quartet online to find their educational backgrounds, personal history, performances, and projects. I printed out (on that mustard-colored paper, *thanks, Jason*) all of this information, studying it on the plane. It is only Eckart whom I have known these past twenty years; the other members have been replaced along the way. In Oregon, I do my best to imagine what kind of people they are, what kind of presents they would like.

Vineta: young and spunky, cutting-edge. I get her a large rubber cuff bracelet made of recycled bike tires cut to look like lace. Also a huge, locally made chapstick, lavender flavored. For Gregor, a sturdily built man who attended university for a year in the States, I get two flavors of peanut butter made by a small company in Portland. Coconut and the cinnamon swirl. For Eckart? He's a man of the world. A hemp bag from my local co-op filled with a combination of Oregonian things like mushroom coffee, bakery fig bars, and organic peanut butter cups.

I arrive at the Musikkindergarten, and it's boisterous, colorful, and chaotic, just like the nature kindergarten I bring my girls to at home. The lady from the office leads me to a large room that has bright blue mats stacked against the side and a whole wall of windows to let in the dingy gray of the Berlin winter.

The first day, we are really getting into it with some trickier repertoire, Shostakovich and late Beethoven. Part of the Beethoven has an esoteric and intellectually complex fugue, and I almost get through it before becoming lost and having to stop. *Uh-oh.* My first big mistake.

Gregor asks:

"What has happened here?"

And I respond:

"Oops, that was me. I had a little 'whooo-hooo.'" Which I accompany with a high-voiced, silly vocalization.

There is complete silence as the three members slowly look at one another. So far, in the five hours that we have played together, no one has cracked a joke. It's quite stark, very different from rehearsing with Jason, where things often careen completely off-topic and random anecdotes are shared.

After about ten seconds, Vineta says, "Well, let's try it one more time, but without your 'whooo-hooo.'"

And she laughs. And after a tick, so do the others. I think it's the first time I have seen their teeth. My goodness. *What a relief.*

That evening we go to a Chinese restaurant down the street, choosing dishes to share. They are surprised that

I am vegetarian, which it's possible to be in Berlin but is essentially impossible as soon as you leave the capital. We talk about the structure of the quartet, expectations, touring schedules, their staff. I am beginning to get a little glassy-eyed from exhaustion, but I remember to pull the presents (not wrapped) out of my orange and black messenger bag. The quartet is surprised, pleased, maybe even a bit confused. Presents must be rare here. They explain that there is a very strict rule of gift giving here. You can't give or receive presents at the university, for example. It's considered a form of bribery.

I say, "Well, in that case, consider yourselves properly bribed!"

And we share our second laugh of the day.

Day two of the audition goes well, and Ecki invites me to his apartment to meet his wife and child, who is about the same age as our younger daughter. He lives in a swanky neighborhood, lots of pre-war apartment buildings interspersed with modern buildings. You see a lot of that in Berlin. Heavy bombing and destruction from fires at the end of World War II mean walking down blocks with a smattering of old buildings visibly pockmarked by artillery and small-arms fire from April and May 1945—the Battle of Berlin. Old buildings and newer construction from the 1950s until today stand side by side. Many blocks still have clear vestiges of bomb craters, gigantic divots in the earth that have been turned into hilly playgrounds and parks.

Ecki's apartment is super modern, very grown-up, white, clean. He has his own practice room and office, the walls lined with awards. There are even fresh flowers in the dining room. I think to myself, *Wow, this guy has a lot of money*. We wait for about twenty minutes, but his wife doesn't show, and we decide to just take a walk.

It's gorgeous around here, with cafes spilling out into the streets, and interesting little stores, and we head into an old brick train station that has been converted into a market, with stalls for butchers, fruit sellers, cheese mongers, and bakeries.

We walk outside for an hour, and I ask him about the finances of the quartet and university, and he asks about my situation. How soon I can extract myself from my obligations and move, if that is what happens. I can move right away. I know how damaging a stagnant concert calendar is for a quartet, and I would not have come if I wasn't willing to rearrange things and start immediately.

I have the next morning off while the quartet discusses. They call to say I have passed to the second round, and if I'm not busy, we could meet in one hour and get started. *Glad I prepared everything in advance.* I am ready to go and meet them at the *Kita* wearing a long-sleeved, above-the-knee purple and blue dress and lavender Uggs that reach to my knees. At home, it seemed quite professional, and I guess it is, for Oregon, but here I look like an absolute hippie. Oh well.

The second round is much more detailed. They challenge me, asking for specific techniques, bow strokes, switching between different philosophies of intonation. Having me demonstrate alone. For a big solo in a Dvořák slow movement, they have me play only with Gregor as Vineta and Eckart go to the other side of the room to watch and listen. It's a delicate solo, rather free, but played against a pulsing rhythm, so the mathematics of the division of note values is tricky, juxtaposed against the freedom and creativity of the line. Control and independence simultaneously. I have a couple of different fingerings and bowings worked out for this one, and I ask if I can try two ways, see which one they like. The second one has a very dangerous, huge shift up, and I decide to take it all on the G string. *Even. More. Dangerous.* But it has a certain quality to it. They love the daring and precision of my second option. They haven't heard it ever played like that before.

In a middle-Beethoven, I suggest a new fingering to Eckart. I have played this piece with Jason a million times and remember a cool fingering given to him by the cellist of the Emerson String Quartet. I suggest it, and we break for the day, leaving Ecki in the room, working on the new fingering.

As I walk into rehearsal the next day, Gregor is active, animatedly pacing. We chat a bit as we wait for Ecki and Vinnie.

As soon as they enter the room, he says:

"I know we haven't had a chance to talk since yesterday. And I know it might feel rushed, but I didn't sleep all night. This is the right choice. Anthea is the right choice. I realize we are supposed to make this decision after tomorrow, and all together, but I am so convinced that I have already set up a photo shoot for tomorrow and a meeting with our manager and publicist today. I don't think we should waste any more time with the audition, but rather we should be practicing for our next concert tours, which start in six weeks."

What??

Eckart and Vineta look at one another and nod. *Yes. They agree. Yes.*

They ask if I accept the position, and I say I just need to check with Jason. He's still at his mom's house; it's late in the evening. I tell him the news, and he is silent. I can hear him taking a really long breath. Like he is bracing for something. Then he asks:

"When do we move?"

We will have three weeks to pack up once I get home. Can he start the process by quitting his university job and the orchestra he conducts? I will call our manager and the pianist of our trio to cancel our concerts.

The rest of the trip goes so fast, I can barely breathe. Radio and newspaper interviews, working with a rental agency to find an apartment, meeting with the managers, publicist, secretary, getting German health insurance and plane tickets for our family, photo shoots. We don't even have time to practice.

And I have to learn six new quartets by the time we move here, for the upcoming tours.

On February 8th, 2016, we fly, all together, to Berlin. We have sold our cars, quit our jobs, gotten rid of our home (glad, in retrospect, that we were renting in Corvallis), found a renter for our vacation house, and given away or donated everything we own besides what can fit in one suitcase each. A small pile of artwork and keepsakes will be shipped later.

Once we arrive, I have to hit the ground at full speed. There are only three weeks before the debut of the new formation, and everything is riding on it. The audition had been warm and friendly, but now the reality is sinking in. Seven-hour rehearsal days, Jason struggling alone as a parent in a new country. And the group is still under a dark cloud. An exhausted cloud that has hung heavily over them since Friedemann's death, nearly enveloping them in a static hopelessness.

The quartet tells me they had been looking for a German man to fill their empty spot. They were not looking for a woman, and certainly not an American woman and mother. Maybe that's why they chose me in the end; maybe I am a breath of surprisingly fresh air in a world that had become thick and claustrophobic. I am exactly what they were *not* looking for. And for the next three years, I am the only American woman in a leading European string quartet, exotic in my down-to-earth, Midwestern, loud, and optimistic self.

A string quartet, that most mysterious and exclusive of beasts, is a rare and magical thing. To enter one, you must have a life's worth of training, experience, the voice of a poet, and nerves of steel. Your education has included daily practice, a slew of demanding teachers, the international competition circuit, deep knowledge of music history and theory, and the ability to develop and share complex emotions with strangers using no words. You are the cream of the crop, and yet you are not satisfied with a position in an orchestra (too regimented, no individuality), not happy to be a soloist (solitary life, solitary voice). You crave the spotlight, but as a member of a perfect cast, a small, intellectually compelling, and flexible collective, with members as obsessed and rigorously trained as yourself. Like a band of super spies.

Since Haydn, who "invented" the genre of string quartet in the late 1700s, the foursome of cello, viola, and two violins has been the darling of composers, the career goal of many string players, the favorite of audiences.

I sometimes think of a string quartet as a solitary person at the piano. Imagine stretching your hands wide, placing them on the keyboard, one to your right and one to your left. Your left hand is the "lower voices" of a string quartet. Your pinky is the cello, deep and powerful. Your thumb is the mellow viola. Now your right hand, the upper voices. Two violins, but with different functions. The thumb of your right hand is the second violin, which is not only a "middle voice" with the violist but also an "upper voice" with the first violin, who is the prima donna of the string quartet: your pinky. That top finger is like the lead singer in a rock band, it's the star. Each of these fingers is like a dancer, able to leap about, taking a solo, a duet, jumping over a partner to overtake their role for a moment. The dancers swirl, pound, glide, alternately hold each other in an embrace, or stand on the edge of the keyboard to deliver a solo.

There are two hundred and fifty solid years of string quartet history, and the works written for the configuration as well as the musicians who perform these works, both past and present, are well known to this day. Classical musicians know by name the most famous performers from the past, even from well before there were recordings. From letters, programs, memoirs, and notes, we know who Brahms wrote his violin concerto for, that person's relationship with Schumann's wife, etc. Music doesn't have a past or present. It's all smashed together.

I wonder if, in two hundred and fifty years, there will be people singing Rihanna songs, getting a PhD in Madonna, or going to a summer seminar where everyone studies and performs Beatles tunes. I know there will be people playing Beethoven and Bach, teaching and learning these historical instruments. Classical music is timeless, endlessly complex, satisfying for both performer and listener. There is nothing like it in the world. People say that classical music isn't that popular anymore (not the case in Europe, and Germany in particular), but there is no arguing about the depth and passion that followers and performers display.

There are string quartets all over the world in every shape and size: from informal groups of friends and college students to professional groups from all countries. But a German quartet, this is something special, something unique. Music is steeped into the culture, beloved by all.

When I'm living in Germany, I am regularly recognized on the streets of cities, asked for autographs in restaurants and airports. Classical music seems to be as popular as rock music; it's their soul, their voice. And the Artemis Quartet, Germany's premiere string quartet, with its four larger-than-life members representing Germany on the world's stages, this is the summit of the art form. An uninterrupted line from Bach himself. The quartet is nothing less than the protector and vanguard of hundreds of years of history through sound, a living representation of the culture of the past and present.

And now, standing and performing inside the Artemis Quartet, I have the same feeling I had watching them play for the first time at Juilliard, twenty years ago. My heart is filled to overflowing with a lifetime of happiness and struggle. I have made it here, to this chance to play in a top string quartet, and to live with my family in Berlin, the capital of classical music. And Jason isn't surprised in the least.

※ 11 *Raven Mother*

The words slip into one another, the language swirling and intertwined. *Rabenmutter*: raven mother; *egoistich*, selfish; *Hausmann*, house husband; *Kinder*, children; *scheiden lassen*, divorce; *aufgeben*, abandon. I nod and smile. I have been hearing this cluster of words for a couple of weeks and despite my lack of basic comprehension in German, I am scooping up the main point. Bad mother. My husband will leave me. I am selfish to have a career.

I am also picking up on the nonverbal cues, the hint of smirky condescension, the almost sincere wish to impart important information, the pity and concern. Emotionally, I am on a pretty intensely erratic roller coaster, giddy from performances, travel, depth of expectations. The after-parties, luxurious treatment, endless parades of wine and adoring fans put me in a hyper-aware state even as they numb my day-to-day existence. And sometimes I am *so* very lonely on tour, even lonely when I come back home, but what do I have to complain about? I am here; I am living my dream. I just need to suck it up and deal with the endless multitude of micro transitions to this new German way of life, which has begun to reveal uncomfortable undercurrents. Where unsolicited advice is freely and strongly given to acquaintances and strangers alike.

My years in Germany were amazing. To be chosen to be the only American woman to be a member of a top European string quartet was a glass-breaking, culture-smashing event of which I am *very* aware. It was in the papers in Germany, I was famous for being selected from a global search, the only violinist from North America even invited to the final rounds in Berlin. But I will be up front here and also say that it was tremendously difficult. I became quite depressed, and the transition to a new culture was surprisingly hard. It was a culture in which I had already spent quite a bit of time previously; I'd even had a serious German boyfriend after Curtis and visited his family in the small city of Mainz. But nothing prepared me for the struggle of becoming more a part of the fabric of the society.

Americans, in the eyes of Germans, are utterly and strangely optimistic, and as a rule they are rule-disregarders and laugh loudly in public, showing their teeth. I have to re-do my driver's license photo because I am smiling with my teeth showing; *unacceptable*! Americans also expect to find happiness through work, are fiercely independent, and say nice things to people, including strangers. It's *outrageous*! When my East German piano partner comes to play concerts with me in Oregon, I go to a tiny coffee drive-through with him. The perky teenage girl serving us is dancing to very loud pop music, and she just *LOVES* my handmade scarf. We chat away about the benefits of scarf-wearing throughout the seasons, agreeing that in our rainy climate it's always a good thing to have a little something to throw over your head if you get caught in our almost-daily dose of sprinkles, how I use mine to carry around my guinea pig in the house, how she signed up for a knitting workshop at the library. She hands me our half-caf chai lattes, and we scoot off down the rainy road. My pianist turns to me and says, "This young person must be a good friend of yours, and you brought me to meet her. She seems kind."

To which I reply, "Oh, I've never met her before."

Looking as if I'm pulling his leg, he says, "But of course you cannot speak to a stranger so much, and for so long. You are kidding with me again, always kidding!"

In Germany, I naturally greet people in stores and on the street, hug colleagues at the university, give gifts to my quartet-mates, and insist my students call me by my first name, instead of *Professorin* Kreston (female Professor Kreston). I start to realize that some people might be insulted by my familiarity or, alternately, charmed by my lack of manners. Germans usually like Americans a lot, finding them silly and funny, but also, I realize, annoying.

On several occasions, I am reamed out aggressively by the woman who owns the gelato store right beneath our apartment in Charlottenburg. We often get her tasty gelato or cakes, and every morning our apartment fills with the smells of almond cakes being baked or poppy seed rolls coming out of the oven. We are good business for her, especially when Jason starts to become known as an excellent teacher for Berlin cellists of all ages, his students stopping by for a gelato before or after lessons. So I assume we are in like Flynn with the gelato lady. As it turns out, I am very wrong.

First it is because the mailman had left a package with her for us to pick up. I'm not sure why she is yelling at me about that, but I just smile and say, "*Danke sehr,*" and take the package. Then it's when I order gelato in cones for my daughters and, as we settle into our little round metal table inside, she hurries aggressively over and gestures firmly. It turns out that cones are only for outside, even in the dead of winter. If you eat inside, it's cups only. *No spilling on the tables!* She makes our small daughters eat their cones over plates, and from then on, always checks with me if we are eating in or going out before filling our orders. I never understand how a business that essentially caters in small doses of messy happiness could have a proprietor who is perpetually in a terrible mood and is a habitual scolder.

All the little things pile up, though.

I am happy sometimes that my German isn't good enough to understand the finer details. Sure, I can pick up on the general flow, but more often than not I am disconnected and I just float. By this point, about half a year into our move to Germany, I have what I would characterize as "airport German." I can get easily from point A to point B, order at restaurants, awkwardly handle official meetings, and flail through meaningless chitchat. Late-night, post-concert dinners start all right, with easy-to-understand references to the concert or repertoire played, but soon I begin to feel like I am surrounded by extras at a movie, all mumbling, "*peas and carrots, peas and carrots*." Staring into space, eyes vaguely crossing, exhausted from the concert and travel, I eat my exquisite meal and wait for someone to engage with me in simplified German, or even better, English. It is during one of these dinners that I first really hear the term *Rabenmutter*. It kind of just meanders about the conversation, running into words like *Mann* and *Kinder* and other things. I just nod and nibble, nod and nibble.

The woman speaking to me is about sixty years old and picks up that I am completely terrible at German and basically just nodding and saying, "*Ja*," or my latest favorite thing to say, "*Stimmt*," which is a catch-all interjection kind of like "totally" or "awesome," every couple of seconds. She switches to perfect English and tells me what's what.

In a nutshell, I am a selfish, shallow woman who is heading for divorce. I had abandoned my kids in order to have a career, leaving them all alone. If my husband hadn't already said he was leaving me, he would soon, and for good reason. It wasn't natural or healthy for a woman with young children to put herself before her husband. Why had I even bothered to have children, when I knew I was going to toss them out of the nest to enjoy my carefree, glamorous life.

OK. *Alright*. Well, that is quite a lot to take in. And even worse, I realize people have been telling me this for months, and I have just been smiling and nodding and trying out my new word, "*Stimmt*." No wonder they think Americans are silly, not-serious people. I don't say anything back to this woman. How could I? She is a high-level patron who has given gobs of money to the concert series that hired us. So I just thank her for her kind words.

The next week I ask my German tutor, Nikolaus, about *Rabenmutter*. He is a serious college student, kind and, with his workbooks and carefully and thoughtfully prepared sheets of nouns and verbs, demanding to a degree that I don't have the time to satisfy. I do my best, but it is obvious that I am disappointing as a student, rarely finishing my assignments. When I mention the word *Rabenmutter*, his normally composed face turns ashen and stern. This conversation is taking place during the part of our session where we talk about German customs and social expectations, an astute suggestion he'd made to help ease my transition into the new world of subtle differences between American and German life. Differences I am beginning to realize are more severe than I had anticipated from my easygoing life in Oregon.

Nikolaus asks where I had heard that word, shaking his head in sadness. He stresses that this is a terrible insult, almost the worst insult someone can say to a woman. A raven is a bird who pushes her chicks out of the nest so that she can release herself from responsibility, he says. In German culture, it refers to either a woman who has decided not to have children to prioritize her career, or a woman who has children but hasn't given up her career to take care of them. *Screwed either way.* People regularly say this to me. People I have never met before. My tutor implores me to ignore these comments, and I explain that as a performer, you are obligated to listen patiently to anyone who wishes to speak to you. You can't talk back or argue. And I certainly don't have the finesse in this new language to engage in a conversation about gender equality.

I also notice, keenly and often, that the two male members of the quartet are never cornered and accused of being terrible fathers. These guys show up at the airport with spouse-packed suitcases, neatly organized and complete with house slippers for backstage, snacks, ironed shirts. They also get picked up and dropped off at rehearsals or the airport or train station in cars warmed and idling, and all the while they are looked at adoringly by their gorgeous wives, hand in hand with their well-maintained and finely groomed children.

I am a pretty good mom. Even now, when my kids are teenagers, we have a lot of hugs, and we can talk about anything. We do fun stuff together, we eat meals together, I support them completely in whatever direction they want to explore. Not that I am perfect, but I am, maybe, *imperfectly* perfect.

Once, in Germany, my youngest is heading out the door for kindergarten, backpack already on, Jason waiting in the car to drive her. She says, "Mom, it's picnic today at kindergarten, did you pack something?" If anything will strike fear into the core of my being it's what to bring to a German picnic or potluck. They're like one of those gorgeous Dutch still lifes of a banquet table overflowing with succulent and sweet platters. Long, thin tables, cheek by jowl with homemade cakes, breads, cheese plates, fruits, and beverages that are made from *actual* recipes.

The foods are labeled with the name of the person who made them and the title of the dish. And I swear, each one is an ancient family recipe handed down through the generations. *Apfelkuchen*, apple cake; *Bienenstich*, bee sting cake; *Mohnkuchen*, poppy seed cake; *Marmorkuchen*, marble cake; *Käsekuchen*, cheesecake; *Pflaumenkuchen*, plum cake; and I can go on. And on. Breads—pumpernickel, Black Forest bread, *Vollkornbrot*, whole grain; *Brötchen*, mixed rolls with seeds on top. I mean, there is a dictionary for the kinds of bread. And let's not get into the meat available.

I am having a panic attack just thinking about those tables. On my best day I'll scramble together a chocolate chip cookie recipe, but, *hold on to your horses*, chocolate chips aren't really a thing over there. You can find them in a specialty store, just like brown sugar, but it's not going to be easy. So it's the old hammer to the chocolate bar to make your own chips. Not a pretty sight.

And so, when my adorable little daughter looks up at me to see what I have prepared for that day, and I look at the clock, realizing I have an airplane to catch in ninety minutes, I unzip her backpack, shove in a watermelon, take a big kitchen knife, wrap it in a dirty kitchen towel, secure it with a hair band, and tuck it inside. As she toddles out the door, bending forward from the weight of that watermelon, I call after her, "There is a huge knife in your backpack, sweetie! See you in four days!"

I know what you are thinking. *Brilliant solution!* I must have gotten a mouthful from the school, had to come in to talk to the principal, maybe even had to deal with an expulsion. But no. *Not a word.* I ask her how her day went on a video call that night, and she says the party was fun, and they appreciated the watermelon. Go figure.

I am perfectly happy to take care of myself, to get to the airport with public transportation. I install a two-person seat on the back of my bike and pedal the girls to school with my violin slung over my shoulder, and then continue on to the university. I take care of my own luggage and all of that, of course. I just don't need a regular list of insults from strangers (who all happen, curiously, to be women) on top of the deep concerns I already have about my responsibility to my family and our precarious balance. As the months continue, and my German improves, I occasionally point out to the person that there are two other members of the quartet who have younger children than I do, and they would probably really enjoy talking about this whole parenting responsibility thing as well. But sometimes I just need to quickly walk away, to have a moment to myself. It is at times like this that I go through the back door and bum a cigarette from a stagehand or kitchen staff, whoever I can flag down. I just need everyone to leave me alone. I am working my butt off, trying to manage one million impossible situations, to be beautiful and say all the right things in a brand-new language, and to be thin, and to be an interesting mom and cook good food and be on time and funny and a good listener and make enough money and do taxes in both countries and manage our rental property in Oregon and learn German and be perfect.

I guess this is just part of the experience, something that will roll off my back. I decide to start to feel sorry for those poor people calling me a raven mother. They must be in terrible relationships, with a lack of mutual respect and support. They must not have confidence in themselves, their partner, or their kids. It must be annoying to be an obnoxious person. And they must not realize that ravens are actually *incredible* creatures. They mate for life, share parenting responsibilities equally, are incredibly intelligent and adaptable, and can do super-duper aerial acrobatics. I decide right there that I like being a raven mother. Yes, I do.

12
Walk Away

The last time I see him is in the emergency room. He's hooked up to all sorts of things and is barely lucid, his eyes watering, his speech slurring. I still can't stomach the idea of touching him, as he feebly holds out his hand towards me. It brings bile up the back of my throat. He embarrassedly apologizes for the smell; he has lost control of his bowels. I wish he didn't apologize for that. It isn't something he is capable of controlling. I do think, however, that he could have apologized for hitting us as children. *That*, he could have controlled. And that also smelled a lot like shit.

We'd gotten a garbled phone call early that morning. The five of us were already in the kitchen making breakfast: me, my mother, Jason, and our two daughters, aged six months and three years. It shows up as my dad on my mom's phone screen; the call isn't understandable, it's like a back-pocket phone call. But there's an ominous tone in it, something that someone is trying to say.

We quickly decide that Jason is going to jump in the car and drive to my dad's office/apartment. My mom calls an ambulance, then heads over in her car as I stay with the kids. It's a seven-minute drive from the family farm in Wisconsin to the small town of Green Lake, where my dad rents a space above a Realtor to be used as an office and, I think, a place to sleep when my parents need space from one another.

Jason is the first to the apartment. It's like a murder scene, he says. A trail of blood and vomit from the kitchen, a plate-sized, dark mass on the floor that looks like a human organ, and a continued line of blood to the bathroom. My father is passed out on the floor, with a large piece of scalp hanging down from his head and blood coming from his mouth down the front of his body. The paramedics are just behind Jason. My dad has thrown up a large part of his stomach, fallen and hit his head on the sink, and managed to call my mom before passing out.

Fifteen years earlier, when we were still graduate students, Jason and I, with an enormous amount of help from my extremely capable mother, started a summer music program in Wisconsin. We were awarded a grant for a rural residency, which gave us the funding for a one-week music program based in the small town of Green Lake. Twelve young people from the surrounding agricultural area were invited to participate, all expenses paid, for private lessons, classes, small ensembles, and concerts.

We cobbled together help from the downtown businesses, leading classes in the bank vault, the library, and the empty holding cell in the basement of the courthouse. Split into three quartets, those young people, who had never had the opportunity for private instruction, grew immeasurably during that week, learning to have confidence in themselves, determination to solve difficult problems, and to work effectively in small groups. The final concert, held in the old opera house, was filled with family and supporters. The students were proudly dressed in their Sunday best, giving their hearts and souls to the music.

It was the first year of a fifteen-year summer institute which grows in length, size, and stature, offering not only free education to young musicians in Wisconsin, but also attracting more advanced students throughout the country. There have been two marriages that started as summer romances at our camp, as well as many young people who continue on to make happy careers in music, from public education to administrative and performance jobs. Funding continues from local organizations and individuals who can see the benefits of a summer arts focus to the area.

Green Lake is the town closest to my grandfather's farm, which he purchased when my mother was a small girl. My parents spend summers and weekends on the farm, renting the pastures and farmable acreage to neighboring farmers. My relationship with my parents is on-again, off-again during these years, complicated by our confusing past. Since I left at age sixteen, we've cycled through periods of guarded closeness, bursts of anger, occasional financial help, and estrangement. Those summer weeks are a neutral meeting ground for us to tentatively and cautiously continue our rocky relationship.

These times are bittersweet for me, because I can feel how damaged we all are. How careful and scared and righteous. Huge fights break out after a week or so. Simmering resentments puncture the thin skin of our family bubble. Accusations, occasional ineffective apologies, some offhand thing that someone says triggers something else. We all walk that tightrope together, feeling the pressure of the other person's pain or anger through our bodies as our weight shifts, trying to stay balanced on the rope that cuts into our feet with every step.

As Jason and I get to know one another better, he begins to hate going to Wisconsin. We started the camp when our relationship was fresh. For years, I don't want to tell him anything about my childhood, just saying things like, "it's tricky," or "lots of complicated stuff went down." I don't want to burden him with my story. I feel that everyone has things they must work through and around. I'm not special. I crave a relationship separate from my damaged past, where I am a whole person, not someone molded by something long ago, but rather crafting my own story, my own present, my own future. My childhood trauma was not my choice, and in choosing to push it away now, I am independent of things that were thrust upon me beyond my control. Even now, if Jason reads this book, there will be more information, more details here than I have ever shared with him.

It's hard for me to see what I am like from the outside. I am so used to the roller coaster of my reactions to memories or anticipated meetings with my family that I don't realize how strongly it affects Jason. Each year, a couple of months before our summer visits, I start to have stomach issues again. The same kind I had as a teenager before I left home. Throwing up, unable to eat, severe pain. I now know how to self-medicate for these periods, taking over-the-counter acid reduction medicines, eating bland foods like toast and scrambled eggs.

I wake myself up at night crying, disoriented and scared. Trying to hide this from Jason, I go to the bathroom to calm myself. But sometimes Jason gently wakes me up, after I call out loudly in my sleep or am shaking and crying. During the day I occasionally irrationally snap or become paranoid, freaking out if the kitchen is dirty or if someone is late. Anything that isn't perfect turns me into a mess, and the things that I think need to be perfect are nonsensical. I think this stems from never knowing what would set my father off when we were kids. It was always something different; you could never predict when or why. I think this is also the reason I strive for personal perfection through my violin playing, never satisfied, *never good enough*.

My episodes increase in intensity and frequency as the visit approaches. Jason eventually insists that we not stay with my parents because it makes everything worse, even more intense. If I wake up and cry during the night at their house, I become scared that someone will hear me, hiding in the bathroom or crying into a pillow. It is a downward spiral.

We begin to stay at the guest house of a donor during the summer camp. Things take a significant turn for the worse when we have our first child. I don't want to have either of my parents alone with her. It's a gut feeling, not attached to any specific fear, but I can't allow it. Not even for a hot minute.

I hire a babysitter to be with our daughter while we are busy teaching and performing. My parents balk and say things like, "We are happy to watch her," "People are asking why you hire a sitter," "Why don't you let us take care of her?" I don't answer. Don't want to open that can of worms. I have enough on my plate with performances, running a camp, and being a mom. I just want to float through these weeks. I think I am being selfish and weak if I don't allow them to at least see her when there is someone officially watching over her.

But the big trouble begins when I have my second baby. My panicked lead-up starts earlier and is more severe than the year before. To complicate matters, I have been having serious postpartum health issues that have me in and out of care. Swelling around the heart and lungs constricts my breathing and causes my heart to race, making me lightheaded and numbing my arms during stressful situations like performance. I take anti-inflammatory medication and they prescribe beta-blockers to keep my pulse low. I am fragile physically and psychologically.

That year we decide to stay at the farm again; my mom can help with cooking, and we will have access to a washing machine. It seems logical, but trying to oversee not only my children but also my parents puts extra stress on my already overtaxed body. Jason does everything he can to help, but I am such a mess. *Huge mess.*

The day of the final camp concert is always intense and exciting. Unexpected small emergencies, the complications of producing a show, performing, managing the onslaught of parents and families, students saying their final, tearful goodbyes, and the immense satisfaction of seeing it all come together. I set up a sitter to stay at the farm with our six-month-old, and a second sitter is supposed to come to the opera house and sit with our three-year-old during the concert. At the last minute she cancels, and I have no choice but to leave Tzippy with my mother as I run around getting ready for the big concert. I tell my mother very clearly, "Stay in the concert hall where I can see you, don't take her outside and don't leave her with Dad." I am as direct as I can be, but somehow, she doesn't understand how literally I mean my instructions.

The concert is halfway over, and I'm making an announcement from the stage. I look out to see my mother sitting next to an empty chair, no Tzippy and no Dad. I'm stuck on stage, and into the microphone I ask my mother, "*Where is Tzippy?*"

She cheerfully points to outside and calls back, "Your dad took her for ice cream."

"Can you go get them now?"

But I can tell she is completely oblivious. I become lightheaded but hold my ground, finishing the concert and rushing outside as soon as it's over.

My dad and Tzippy are walking up the street, from the direction of his office. I run to see her, noticing the remnants of chocolate ice cream on her face. She says, "Grandpa took me to his office."

My whole body begins to shake as I take her in my arms, carrying her back to the opera house. Why can't my parents just follow simple directions? Why don't they see what is happening to me? How blind are they? *How blind have they been for my whole life*? Why does this never stop? When will it stop? *I just want it to stop.*

I find Jason, quickly looking down to hide my eyes swelling with suppressed tears, trying to calm my breathing. I feel embarrassed at my reaction. Of course nothing happened. I ask Tzippy what she and my dad did together and she says, "We got ice cream and I drew on paper at the office." Okay. Okay.

After cleaning up the hall and saying goodbyes to the students, we head back to the farm for dinner. I feel like I am in a cloud, but as usual, I hide my condition as best as I can. I always feel like it is my own problem, something I have to deal with, and I don't want to burden people when they are actually doing nothing wrong. I don't want to punish people for past wrongs, but I am desperate to prevent a *future* wrong.

We sit around the kitchen after I pay the babysitter and breastfeed Mirabai, our younger daughter. It's just mild chit-chat, talking about the concert and how the camp went. Things we will keep the same for next year, things we will change. I don't know if I am hypersensitive—well, actually, *of course* I am hypersensitive—but my dad is interacting a lot with Tzippy. I hear him say, "Do you want to stay with me at the office tonight, have a sleepover?" I say, firmly, "That won't happen. No sleepovers." My stomach starts to hurt, and I lay down on the cold, Formica-tiled floor. Closing my eyes, I drift in and out of conversation as dinner is coming together. Tzippy comes over and asks if she can have a sleepover. I say *absolutely not*. We can go over together tomorrow, though, before we leave. I hear my dad ask her two more times if she wants to come over, and again I say no. "No, no sleepovers, no."

Looking back on it, so many strange behaviors in our family were normalized. Why didn't anyone help me off the kitchen floor and into the other room? Or maybe they tried, and I was too stubborn, fighting against my own body, refusing its sickness. It's what we had gotten used to, what *every family* gets used to. Covering up or hiding. The little secrets, the big secrets.

My stomach gets so bad I eventually leave the kitchen, taking the kids with me to bed, and my dad leaves, too. Neither of us has eaten dinner. He's going to sleep at the office again. It's just me, my mom, Jason, and our daughters remaining at the farm.

That night, I wake with terrors, crying and shaking. I try to keep quiet, but I am as upset as I have ever been. I decide at that moment to wake my mother up. To show her what is happening to me. To make it as real to her as it is to me. I stand by her bed, crying, and she sits up, worried, asking me what is wrong.

I can't speak, just stand there, heaving. She gets up and we go to the bathroom, I guess for tissues. I finally say something like, "This is what it's like for me. This is how I feel and this happens. This happens a lot."

She says, "Why, why does it happen?"

And I reply, "Because of *everything* that happened. It

gets worse and worse the closer I get to coming here, and it takes months to get back to normal after I leave."

She is caring, putting her thin arm around me. It doesn't feel particularly soothing. We don't have a family that touches each other and it's more jarring than helpful. It makes me squeamish. She honestly seems to have no idea what I am talking about. What I would be upset about. She is bewildered.

That dark, nighttime conversation is the closest I have ever come to being honest with her. I let her see me without my guard up, with no protection. We never mention that night again, and in the morning, when that garbled call comes from my father, I can see it all. *He and I are the same.* Torn apart from the inside out. Damaged. For different reasons, but for the same reason. His near-death experience is as close as I will ever get to an apology from him. An acknowledgement. It is from deep inside of him, not from his mind or through words. But that dark, bloody mess that erupts from him is the embodiment of everything that has gone wrong. A blob of evil comes out of him that day, but I know there is more still inside of him. And he can't change. Can't change. He is never going to be around my children again.

He doesn't deserve to know them.

That day, I walk away from him forever.

Later, I am diagnosed with post-traumatic stress disorder, but it has mostly disappeared now. It comes back when I see my mother, and Jason tells the girls, "Grandma is coming for a visit, so Mama will start to act funny again. She might yell or decide to stay in a hotel. But don't worry, she'll be back to normal in a week or two."

Yes, back to normal. Gosh that sounds good.

It's mid-March 2025, and I've just finished writing this chapter, "Walk Away." I'd made the decision to write it while Jason is gone on a two-week concert tour of Germany, when I'll have more space and privacy to process it all, to take my time. I am strong enough. Ready.

I start to write as I always start to write, thinking about the topic as I jog, while practicing, sleeping. I make lists, figure out how everything is intertwined. No matter how much the narrative can be steered, something else takes hold, something I can't control. I am not able to see these events as completely in the past, because my body and mind feel my memories as if they are happening right now. Writing this chapter becomes an obsession. "Walk Away" is my every waking and sleeping moment during these two weeks, pulling me down into a deep despair, suffocating. I relive those moments over and over again. I know there will always be these visceral memories that threaten my foundation. But it is up to me to decide how to react. *Or that's what I believe at the time, anyway.*

It is a busy fortnight for me, not just being a mom, but also rehearsals in Portland, five quartet concerts, and a lecture for the Oregon Symphony. When I get to the university for the first rehearsal, I have a sharp pain in my chest. I assume it is something I tweaked during the two-hour drive. I pop an ibuprofen and hunker down for five hours of violin playing.

As the day continues, it begins to feel like something dark is growing inside me. Pushing out against my ribs, stretching them apart, causing me to catch my breath; I am unable to bend from the waist for fear of a sharp pain, something trying to get out. Like a finger is hooked around my rib, prodding and poking.

Six months earlier, I had joined my first writing group.

The four of us become shockingly close, learning about each other's lives in ways we don't share with anyone else. The mistakes and dreams and longings. We are more than a writing group. We are a support for one another, asking uncomfortable questions, urging each other to dig into our honesty and to discover deeper levels of our own truths.

These women each have a lifetime of stories. One woman is publishing the story of a long-ago relative who bravely emigrated from a small island north of Germany to Texas as a young woman in the 1800s. Another is recounting her life as a single mother of three, living by her wits with courage and humor. Another writes about the beauty of a life shattered by mental struggle, leading to electroshock treatment that emptied her mind of the past. A memoir with no memory, only old journals to fill in the holes. And there is me, a story of adventures, disappointments, and triumphs, fought for and won.

They patiently urge me to share more of what happened between me and my father, asking questions such as:

"Do you still speak?"

"Is he alive?"

"Where was your mother?"

They encourage me to write about it when I find the fortitude. Even if it is a story that I will not share with anyone else. *For me alone.* It is a part of me, a piece of dark thread that is woven into the fabric of my life, despite the fact that I push it away, ignore it, and deny its strength.

As my chapter grows, so does my pain. My memories spread like a sick web from childhood to that fateful day in Green Lake, just as my chest pain radiates to my back and up my shoulder, feeling like it is punching me or choking me from inside. It is impossible to sleep;

I begin to be nauseous, taking antacid medication and barely eating. I drive myself to urgent care. They think it is probably a pulled muscle, nothing to worry about. But it continues to worsen.

I don't like it when something or someone tries to dictate what I should do, how I feel, how I am supposed to act. Not only do I not like it, I absolutely *refuse* to comply. I'm as stubborn as it gets. It's *my life* I am living. It's my life I have fought for and my life that I love. This pain in my chest feels like it is coming from somewhere else, someone else. It isn't *me* who is sick; it is something else trying to make me sick, and I do not agree.

I am playing concerts this whole time, driving several hours each day, rehearsing, performing, and driving home. Not sleeping, taking three ibuprofens at a pop. The day after I finish writing "Walk Away," I can't even wear a bra anymore because of the pain, and don't feel well enough to drive the girls to school. They just skip the day. I go to the urgent care again, bringing a copy of this chapter so I can edit while I wait. They don't even admit me this time, immediately sending me to the emergency room. The doctor asks if I have ever felt this way before, and I say it reminds me of how I felt after I had my second child. Lightheaded and weak, unable to breathe, pain throughout my chest like I have been sucker-punched, only able to eat toast. After an EKG, a blood test comes back showing the likelihood of a blood clot. They run a series of tests. I am okay, but I have swelling around my lungs that is pushing on my chest cavity from inside, constricting breathing and causing my heart to flutter.

The day after the ER visit, I become suddenly irrational, upset at my older daughter for leaving a dirty pan in the kitchen after she was supposed to clean. I don't yell. I cry and am shaking a little, asking, "Why don't you care about me? You can see I am in pain, why don't you help me?"

With wide open eyes, she sweetly apologizes and the girls and I start a deep clean of the kitchen, from mop to stovetop, all three of us together. *Why did I do that?* What is wrong with me? I am not a monster. *I don't do things like that!* I ask for her forgiveness, we talk, we hug.

Jason returns the next day from his tour, both exhausted and refreshed. He is very concerned about my health. I tell him I wrote about that day in Green Lake, and he says, "Well, can't you see? You sent yourself to the hospital. You gave that chest pain to yourself by writing that chapter! I mean, it's good to write it, if you want to, but you're killing yourself. You can't eat and you can't sleep, and you feel like throwing up all the time, and you get upset when there is a dirty pan in the kitchen and then yell at our daughter. It's a classic Anthea freak-out."

I close my eyes, looking inside myself to find the truth, searching for the answers. I slowly smile, then start to laugh. We are hugging each other and rocking in a circle in the dirty kitchen. Our messy home, filled with toast and antacids and a pottery wheel and guinea pigs and kids and laughter and music and love. The life that I have created for myself, and the life that has been created around me and because of me is my choice. This is the life I embrace. And it feels really, really good to be here, right now, a member of this most remarkable, caring family. I can't ask for anything more.

※ 13
An Epic Love Story

Aspen, Colorado. 1997. I am twenty-four years old. Attending the celebrated Aspen School of Music for nine weeks. I am the violist of the Avalon String Quartet, and along with the Miro String Quartet, we are eight of six hundred students from around the world. But really, we are unique, because the rest of the summer camp is involved in a rigorous daily schedule, mostly orchestra and opera rehearsals. My quartet is expected to make our own rehearsal schedule and to set up lessons with the faculty. We've been selected from international auditions to come here for free, with accommodation, food, lessons from major quartet musicians, master classes, and high-profile concerts. We've just come off of our Carnegie Hall debut and a couple of big competition wins and are feeling strong, powerful and invigorated.

I've been living in DeKalb, Illinois, between year one and two of my quartet's residency with the Vermeer Quartet, a renowned group with a detailed and demanding approach to teaching the discipline of a life as a string quartet. We'd moved there from Cleveland the year before, and I am in a pretty feisty mood, generally.

I'm looking for a way to easily supplement my income,

which leaves me scrambling to pay my rent and car insurance, my bank account with a negative balance at the end of every month. I am living in an illegal loft space in an old sewing machine factory lazily partitioned with flimsy walls, which is above a raucous pool hall on the main street of town, across from a dive bar, and next to a Thai restaurant. My space is just a gigantic cube, and someone before me built a rickety loft in the corner. It's about ten feet high, with a ladder. I somehow get my mattress up there, but there is no railing so I have to be careful to not accidentally roll off in my sleep.

There are seven living spaces of different shapes on the second floor, and we share one bathroom at the end of the hall that has a toilet, loosely bolted to the floor, a wobbly sink, and a disgusting shower. We also have a kitchen, which has a hodgepodge of nonworking items, like a broken stove and a hot refrigerator, plus a bold colony of cockroaches. *Best to be avoided.* Both the bathroom and kitchen.

I make my own kind of kitchen inside my space, attaching boards to the wall with brackets to create a shelving area, with a slow cooker, mini fridge, burner, and toaster. A bucket for clean water and a bucket for dirty dishes that I bring into the kitchen to wash by hand every day.

I love to throw dinner parties along a table that I cobble together from a couple of card tables and a big piece of salvaged plywood I found on the street. I drape blankets and sheets over it to make it look fancier. I make lentil soup and roasted vegetables, hummus, tzatziki, and sesame breadsticks. After dinner, we drink, smoke, and play massive games of Twister. I have a rabbit (Chester) and a lovebird (Aphrodite). They are more or less free range. There are salvaged couches around, a television, bookshelves made from boards and concrete blocks, and

I have turned the bottom of the loft into an immense walk-in closet.

I have a stipend from school, occasional checks from my mother, and I play in the Rockford Symphony Orchestra. Between these things and some quartet gigs, I can almost manage every month. I make some signs, advertising violin lessons for $25 an hour, and post them around town in coffee places, the library, thrift store. I finally get a bite. He plays violin, but not very well, and would like to have a couple of lessons to refine his technique. I give him my address and we set up a meeting time.

The front door to the loft apartments is currently bashed in, with shards of glass hanging from the frame. There is someone living illegally in the hallway upstairs by the bathroom, so I have to hold it, going to the restroom at school, using the shower at the rec center. Our landlord, who owns the pool hall below, is a drunk and doesn't fix anything, ever. I do my best to sweep up the glass in preparation for my new student, but it's pretty hazardous to get through the door so I just wait for him out front.

I don't know what my student looks like, and it's a couple of minutes past the hour. A motorcycle parks in the alley to the side of the pool hall, and as the guy gets off his bike, pulling his helmet off and shaking his long, blond hair, I notice he's got a violin case. He's also gorgeous, by the way, wearing black leather pants. *Oh my God.*

I lead him around the back of the building and up the rusty fire escape. It turns out he is the violinist of The Danglers, a punk/heavy metal band with an Irish influence. Pretty popular around here. Big stage persona. He plays violin and sings; there is also an upright bassist and a drummer. Three guys. His name is Jason Loveall, but people call him Captain Loveall, or just Cap'n.

Okay just stop right there. *Just stop it.* Obviously, we get together. He's funny, kind, likes to party, and absolutely adores me. He woos me, old-school style. Slowly. With mixtapes he makes for me, poems, dropping me off at school on the back of his bike. He comes to hear me play the Sibelius *Violin Concerto* with an orchestra and cries afterwards. The entire left-hand side of his beautiful body is scarred from a major motorcycle accident a couple of years before. Little pieces of glass and gravel work their way up to the surface regularly, and we open his skin and pull them out together.

Lessons go well; he's at about Suzuki book two level, doesn't know how to shift out of first position or vibrate, doesn't really know how to read music. He's a high school dropout, like the rest of the band, like the rest of his family. He's got a really cute dimple and blue eyes.

He lives in a similarly illegal setup above the thrift store down the street, and when the cops come and shut it down, he moves into my place. I go to a lot of his shows; it's similar to Luna, my old Cleveland band, but it's raucous and manly and headbanging and the bars are nasty and it feels dangerous, in a really good way.

No one in Captain Loveall's family has ever had a career, and I slowly start to talk to him about his future. Playing in this band is great, but what about in ten years? Twenty? What about college? What if I talk to my violin professor and see what kind of scholarships are available? In the meantime, I put him through the wringer. Ševčík études, introducing the positions, scales, Mozart *3rd Concerto*, discipline, and a daily practice schedule. Which is pretty hard because he's usually hungover, gets back some point between dawn and lunch, and loves to drink heavily, not to mention the drugs.

I talk to my professor, a quiet, serious German violinist. We have patient and detailed lessons, discussions on the history of certain fingerings or the study of bow pressure and speed combined with angle. Interesting stuff. Meticulous. I explain my situation. I have a student who is a terrific performer with amazing stage presence and passion, who stopped lessons in grade six. I am working on the basics, hand structure, intonation, style, and technical proficiency. He has absolutely no money. Is there a scholarship?

In the summer, I have to leave DeKalb for the Aspen Festival, and Loveall stays to house-sit, taking care of my animals and promising to bring my signed checks to the utilities office and send in the phone checks also. We split the cost of a Greyhound bus to Aspen so he can visit in a month.

In Aspen, things go well. We are practicing hours and hours every day, working with the Emerson Quartet. It's the beginning of a long and important relationship; in two years we will follow them to the University of Hartford to study with them.

I eat in the cafeteria every day, perched on the side of a hill overlooking the quaint but ritzy ski town of Aspen. Nestled in a valley in the Rocky Mountains, Aspen is an old silver mining town, walkable and charming, ski resorts surrounding the valley. Its inhabitants are both the extremely wealthy and the less affluent local ski bum community. So you can still get a slice of pizza for a couple of bucks or a burrito, despite the five-star restaurants and glittering resorts. One day, I am standing in line at the burrito place, and the guy in front of me has forgotten his wallet. He's cracking jokes like wildfire and ends up digging a checkbook out of his back pocket. He writes one for the burrito, and they immediately pin it to the wall. It's Steve Martin—and this isn't the only time I see him that close. Stay with me for a second.

Jump ahead five years, and Jason and I are playing in a festival in the French West Indies, on St. Barths. We have been coming here for three years, staying for two weeks in this Caribbean paradise to play concerts in the historic colonial churches with a group of around twenty musicians from various nations. Leonard Nimoy (Spock from *Star Trek*) lives here most of the time and enthusiastically attends concerts. Jason borrows a cello from Bruce Paltrow, an amateur cellist who also lives on this island. He's Gwyneth's dad. Jason and I are staying with a French family who have become dear friends over the past three years. They live in the middle of the tiny island, with chickens and a house they built entirely by themselves. It is composed of individual, freestanding little rooms surrounding a small but deep swimming pool. They began with just one room and added as they could afford new materials. They bring us to midnight parties on hidden beaches accessible only by dinghy, filled with locals, bonfires, and music. The rides there are in pitch black, the waves large. We hold on for dear life to the bouncing, rubbery sides of the raft, coming back by the light of the dawn.

After an afternoon concert one day, we drive our golf cart to the house to drop our instruments and change for the beach, wanting to enjoy a couple of hours of off-time before the evening concert. But we can't find our keys to the gate! We decide to just head to the ocean anyway, and as we crest the dunes to go to a secluded spot, Jason with his tuxedo and cello, me with my floor-length silk dress and violin, we come face-to-face with Steve Martin, coming out of the water. We all freeze for what feels like ten minutes, staring at each other. I turn to Jason and say, "Take out your cello, let's play Czardas."

In my mind, this moment can change the trajectory of my entire life. But Jason is overwhelmed with admiration. He simply can't do it and we all turn away: Steve back to the ocean and us to the shade of the windswept bushes to the side of the beach. If I can pinpoint one regret I have in my *entire* life, it's not taking my violin out right at that moment, walking towards the ocean, and serenading Steve Martin.

Back to Aspen. And the love story.

I am sitting at a long table in the cafeteria eating lunch with my quartet and a random other guy who knows the cellist in my quartet. She introduces him as Jason. He's tall, six-foot-five, with dark hair and a dimple on his chin. He's pretty hilarious. My cellist turns to me: she has a huge crush on him from before but is too shy to ask him out. Can I ask him to meet the two of us at a bar tonight? Can I come as her wingman, then disappear when the moment is right? Sure. I'm not shy. I ask him and we set a place and time. He's the solo cellist of the seven-piece contemporary ensemble, which is the only other scholarship group at Aspen that summer. They hold national auditions and only have one cello spot. It's a pretty high-profile gig.

We meet at a basement bar; it's dark and quiet and a bit fancier than I am comfortable with. Like, $18 drinks. We chat and it starts to become obvious that he has accepted the invitation not because of my quartet cellist, but because of me. I am not interested or available. I have Captain Loveall already. Can't really top that.

I excuse myself, but there he is the next day at the cafeteria. He comes to hang out with the quartet that night for cards and gin and tonics, and he shows us a game that gets us all laughing so hard it's painful. I have to clutch my side and am rolling on the floor.

I go outside for a smoke and he follows me. It's obvious what's going on here. But I don't have time for this. I am super busy with quartet and my life.

So I say to him, "Okay, we can make out, but I'll give you only ten minutes. I have an early rehearsal tomorrow morning and want to get a good night's sleep. Let's see what you've got."

The next day, I am walking downtown, and he happens to see me across the street. He waves and I wait. He asks me where I am going and I say to the public library to get a temporary card.

He's like, "Oh, I'm headed there too—what kind of books do you like to read?"

What a turn-on.

He picks out *To the Lighthouse* by Virginia Woolf and Italo Calvino's *Baron in the Trees*. I get Thomas Mann's *Buddenbrooks* and A.S. Byatt's *Possession*. He invites me for a hike the next day; he'll bring lunch. I pick him up in my painted Buick Skylark, and we head to the Maroon Bells. We eat baguette, cheese, and wine in a meadow filled with wildflowers.

I was idly recollecting his very impressive ten-minute audition the other night, and I don't know what happened exactly, but we haven't been apart since that day. It's been twenty-eight years. It was a passionate summer, rivaling *Pride and Prejudice* in its veiled secrecy and palpable desire. We hid our affair from my quartet, necessitating sneaky early-morning escapes from my dorm room so that my colleagues wouldn't see him. Furtive handholding under the table, brushing against one another accidentally while walking. I start to make excuses to the quartet for why I can't hang out in the evenings. I decide to go to see one of Jason's shows.

I am very nervous to see Jason play for the first time. What if he is terrible? Cold and shallow? Sloppy technique? Awkward on stage? It's almost better to not even go. I very likely will have to break off our secret affair after a disappointing concert. I can't stay with a player I don't respect. And I am currently living with an amazing performer, one who would be difficult to top . . . and who I hope is taking care of my rabbit and bird and not just having huge parties at my place.

I show up at Harris Hall, a five-hundred-seat subterranean Greek-styled concert hall. A modern, asymmetrical wooden backdrop surrounds the performers on stage. Jason's seven-piece contemporary ensemble is playing a concert of newly composed and avant-garde works. There is a piece for amplified cactus, a couple of larger works that are so complex they need a conductor even though there are only seven performers. And then Jason has a solo piece. He walks confidently on stage, holding his cello in front of him, bowing to the warm applause. Sitting alone on that big stage, he starts tenderly, weaving a haunting line at the top of his instrument. Working his way down, he becomes a wild animal, attacking the instrument with violent, repeated downbows. Ending with lilting sounds of nature, he stands to the rush of applause. *Yes. He'll do.*

Captain Loveall arrives the next week at the Denver Bus Station, a three-hour drive from Aspen, and I pick him up in my car. We visit a friend of his, Little Fyodor, who is half of the experimental performance duo Little Fyodor and Babushka. They are a big part of the underground music scene in Denver, unconventional and just plain weird. They perform in costume, songs like "Dance of the Salted Slug" and "Slither/Sloth." We are going to a bowling alley/music venue to hear the band.

The crowd that night is odd. Very different from The Danglers' gigs, which are attended mostly by bikers and leather-wearing guys drinking beer and hard liquor. The bowling alley is filled with the pot-smoking alternative crowd. Hats with plumes, crocheted dresses, colored drinks with fruit. Intellectuals. *I realize in that bowling alley that I am in love with both Jasons.* Jason Loveall *and* Jason Duckles.

I am a natural multitasker. Surely I can manage this? Jason (cellist) knows I have a live-in boyfriend but he doesn't care, or is happy to just have a great summer. I know Captain Loveall is into me, but I don't think he can even imagine what a monogamous relationship means. It's clear from his general way of being that he doesn't believe in that kind of thing. But still, he doesn't know about Jason, and I am afraid that he is too fragile to handle it, so I decide to keep it hidden.

For the next week, Cap'n Loveall lives with me while I sneak out to see Jason, meeting him at his hotel or the burrito place. I'm excellent with schedules and partitioning my life, and I am feeling pretty good about how it's going. It's exhausting and busy, but I can do it. We even meet all together at a bar: the quartet, Captain Loveall, and Jason. I am sitting between them and it's a bit difficult to manage the under-table activity but I succeed with flying colors, or that's what I think, anyway. That night, Loveall is suspicious and reserved. He decides to go out by himself, late. I see him the next day, clearly in a drug hangover. He says he met some people down by the river and they did some heroin. Alright. Fine. No problem.

I meet Jason that afternoon, and as we walk down the street, he grabs my hand. I hear some kind of animal howl behind me, and turning, I catch a glimpse of Loveall rounding the corner. Oh no. When I get back to my room, it's been destroyed. He's cut up my favorite pair of corduroys and tacked them to the wall, spelling the word *WEAK*. There are lipstick messages all over the bathroom walls and mirror, stream of consciousness poetry kind of stuff. Dark. Everything ransacked, his stuff gone. I am worried about him and I don't want to see him in pain.

I don't see him for three days. He shows up at my door, dirty and disheveled. He's been living down by the river and is super high. I take him gently into my arms, and he says he is heading back to DeKalb. I walk him to the bus station, paying for his trip to Denver and giving him twenty dollars for food.

When I get back to DeKalb, my apartment is in pretty good shape. The phone and electricity are cut off, but the animals are alive. When I see Loveall he says he crossed out the words and used the utility checks for booze. That's okay. My neighbors say that the parties he has been throwing are massive; they saw a guy with nothing but a pair of cowboy boots on walking down the hall. The sink in the bathroom has been pulled away from the wall.

A year later, Captain Loveall passes his high school equivalent exam and enters college on a full scholarship specifically reserved for a local student. He studies with my German violin professor, gets a music education degree, and has been teaching music in the public schools in Milwaukee since graduating. We are still in touch; we exchange warm messages every couple of years. He has a daughter he named Viola, after me.

And as for me and Jason? Our natural compatibility on and off stage begins to weave our lives together. For the first time in my life, I find someone who I love both as a musical partner and a companion, who I can laugh and travel with. Who dreams as big as I do. We make each other better versions of ourselves, and our chemistry during concerts is palpable. Our love story continues to this day, and sometimes when we are driving in the car with the girls, Jason will point to a guy with long hair, dressed in leather, and say, "Hey girls, look, it's an ex-boyfriend of Mama's!"

That summer was truly my summer of love.

And it's that love that carries me through life. Through all of it. The happy moments are shared with abandon, and the sad moments have the space to sink in. Jason is by my side, as are the two absolutely lovely teenagers we created together. Our family quartet. It's like the four of us are all molding each other, every day, all of the time.

𝄐

At this moment, I'm fifty-four, living back in Corvallis, Oregon. I suppose this means that I am mid-middle-aged. In any case, I am perimenopausal—or maybe on Tuesday, when I see my gynecologist, she will finally tell me I am menopausal and I can get started on the last third of my life. Which is going to be fabulous, by the way.

I play first violin in the Delgani String Quartet. And the instrument I play on? Yes, my grandfather's violin, found and returned by the police in Germany a mere ten weeks after it was stolen. Mirabai, our younger daughter, plays on my mother's old Italian violin. She's pretty into it, entering competitions and sitting first chair of her youth orchestra. Every Sunday we take a pilgrimage to see her teacher, a vivacious seventy-eight-year-old. She's an actively concertizing violinist, one of the last living students of the legendary Russian virtuoso Jascha Heifetz, and she lovingly teaches our daughter the importance of finding her own voice.

The documentary I was hoping to be a part of? The Dutch documentarian Hester Overmars followed the Artemis Quartet for an entire year, and the resulting documentary, *The Neverending Quartet*, portrays the Artemis in a turbulent year when Ecki and I decide to leave the quartet. The recording we make that same year wins the *Diapason d'Or*, France's highest honor for classical music. During my years in Berlin, I was invited to play with the Berlin Philharmonic and as a guest concertmaster of the Deutsche Oper Berlin. A colleague at the University of the Arts became a dear friend, and together with Jason we began a new trio, which still enjoys touring and recording in Germany.

In the early days of the pandemic, I started an online music academy, the first of its kind. I have had thousands of students, employed over seventy musicians, and made enough money to buy our dream house on the top of a hill surrounded by deer and wild turkeys. The story of the academy and the help it offered to isolated young people and musicians throughout the world came to the notice of the *New York Times*, who ran a feature. The academy continues today, both online and in a historic theatre in downtown Corvallis, attracting students of all ages from all over the United States. The academy keeps us busy year-round, works with our somewhat erratic schedules, and gives us a chance to continue teaching the great chamber music repertoire that was so lovingly taught to us by wonderful teachers from Isaac Stern to the Emerson String Quartet.

Those hot flashes and sleepless nights? Yes, disrupting and erratic, but just a part of every woman's journey. Not too dissimilar from those pregnancy and baby years, in a crazy-making, up-and-down, out-of-control kind of way. And a nice accidental benefit is that a lot of this book has been written during those menopause-induced insomniac nights, waking up after just a couple of hours of sleep to silent, pitch black in which I can wander the house and ruminate with a mug of warm tea. Home alone in a house full of happily sleeping people.

My aging body? I embrace my wrinkles, a sign of hard-earned wisdom. So what if I gained fifteen pounds along the way. No danger of me turning into a translucent bird. My hair is slowly morphing into silver; in a couple of years I will be sporting a mop of mottled gray curls, and that's going to be pretty sweet. I'll probably start to have incredibly painful and debilitating arthritis like my mother, curling my fingers in and making my knuckles look like cauliflower, but I figure, "Hey, guess who doesn't have to practice violin anymore?"

I try to go to the athletic club a couple of times a week, more if I have an off-week with no quartet rehearsals. Pilates, weight training. Yoga with Bruce. He's about my age and a foot shorter, with a rather substantial belly, wispy beard that reaches past his collarbone, and wavy hair that nearly meets the length of his beard. Usually tied in a bun or tail, but this past week it was out. Flowing and free. He carries a large woven basket to class, overflowing with a scarf, mat, CDs for the day. His verbal encouragements are somehow both standard, like those self-help posters on the wall at the dentist, and also entirely heartfelt, touching, and welcoming. When I bring my older daughter, she is either rolling her eyes at me, giggling uncontrollably, or just taking a nap on her yoga mat. I think that's why she doubles up on mats. I love Bruce, his affirmations, his whispered encouragements as he glides around the room, as light as air. The generous rectangle of belly that appears and disappears as we do our upward and downward salutes. Owning it. My favorite? When he decides to read vaguely depressing poetry, very slowly and quietly, after we do our alternate nostril breathing, lying on the floor in our restful poses.

I have a life now that my oldest daughter calls "refreshingly uneventful." Maybe I am that lion that Hong told me about in Kazakhstan, reserving my energy for the next big pounce, or maybe this is just the new me. The chilled-out me.

I can't imagine what more there is to have, what *all* there can be in a life, but I am ready. If life is a crescendo, I am only halfway there.

Acknowledgments

This dream of writing a book, which never occurred to me would be a possibility, could not have happened without all of you. And to be able to share these memories with the people who created them with me makes this all the sweeter.

To Jason. How can I even start. You have been my best friend, partner in music and life, and supporter since day one in that cafeteria in Aspen. None of any of this would be possible without your selfless giving, humor, and hard work.

Mirabai and Tzippora. I am so lucky to share a life with you. You have read every word of this book, asking questions that deepened the story, and in this way, we have gotten to know each other on a deeper level than I would have ever anticipated. You trust me, laugh at me, and hug me all at once.

With appreciation to my family of origin—our journey together created a path forward for me, filled with daring and adventure.

To my teachers, Almita and Roland Vamos, the Emerson Quartet (Phil Setzer, Eugene Drucker, Lawrence Dutton and David Finckel), Ida Kavafian, Wu Han, Isaac Stern and Felix Galimir. Your thoughtful, demanding and inquisitive teaching always pushed me to be a better musician. To ask the questions the music asks of us, to be powerful and tender, to be honest and never satisfied. You taught me obsession. Your teaching is with me every day, and I speak of you all, all of the time.

Fred Child—in the early days, you shined a light on me, and showed me that music is much more than just a performance, that it's an investigation into the mysteries of humanity. Our time in D.C., Italy, and now in Oregon gives me a chuckle. You encourage me to think big, stretch my arms wide, and see what I can create.

Yo-Yo! Your warm laugh, attentive listening, and flexible mind are a wonder to be around. Being close enough to smell the rosin lifting in a cloud from your bow makes me feel like I have been anointed by a unicorn. Thank you for believing in me.

To Norman Lebrecht, who saw something in me that no one else had ever seen. That I could write. That I loved it. And your steady friendship and belief in me are the reason I am typing these words out right now, on my phone with my thumbs, just like I typed this whole book. And why I won't ever stop.

Eugene Drucker, teacher, mentor, and supporter. Thank you for the advice and encouragement, in music, life, and writing. Your example of a life that encompasses many different passions is an inspiration.

Isabelle Bleecker and Nordlyset Literary Agency. Before we had our first meeting, I turned to Jason and I said "this next hour might change my life forever." And it has, in spades. Thank you for believing in me, for guiding and advising me, and for pushing me in the direction I needed to go. I am learning so much, and loving every second of it. Thank you for taking a chance on me.

I am so grateful to be a part of the Paul Dry Books family. From Paul, who trusted that my voice would solidify, to Julia Sippel, editor extraordinaire, who helped my words flow and dance, and Mara Brandsdorfer, publicity maven, I am cared for, challenged, and improved. I can't believe how lucky I got with you all!

Ling Ling Huang. Your astute advice, clear-headed ambition and strength was a game-changer for me. I am in awe of your talents and determination.

Blair Tindall, who is no longer with us, thank you for your help in the early days. Reading my diary, sharing your first book proposal with me, reviewing my very first draft. Your spunky comments and freedom on the page encouraged me to be exactly who I am.

To Ann, Stephanie, Joann, and Nilly, my Willamette Writers Saturday group. You have been with me from chapter one. I wouldn't have gotten to the finish line without you.

Artemis, Avalon, and Delgani quartets, Amelia Piano Trio, and Thunder Egg Consort, thank you for sharing your lives with me, and creating something together that is uniquely our own. I have learned so much from you all; you made me a better musician, listener, and human.

For all those who read a chapter or more and offered encouragement and advice, your input gave me the courage to forge ahead, making time and space to find my voice. And thank you to my students and their families, past and present, for always making my day a little bit better than I thought it could be.

A Reader's Guide to *Crescendo* by Anthea Kreston
is available at pauldrybooks.com.

About the Author

Photo by Christine Dong

Anthea Kreston is a world-renowned violinist and violist who has performed on almost every major concert stage around the globe, including Carnegie Hall, Lincoln Center, the Kennedy Center, the Royal Academy of Music (London), Prince Regent Theatre (Munich), Teatro Nacional (Panama City), and Château d'Ainay-le-Vieil, among many others. She has played in the Berlin Philharmonic, as Principal Violin in the St. Paul Chamber Orchestra, as concertmaster of the Deutsche Oper Berlin, and with Yo-Yo Ma's Silk Road Project.

An avid writer, Kreston is a frequent columnist for the music news site Slipped Disc. She has published articles in classical publications such as

Strings and *Chamber Music Magazine* and has been featured in the *New York Times*, *Strings*, and *Strad* magazine for her work with students during COVID, community building through music, and music therapy with abused children.

Kreston is currently first violinist of the Delgani String Quartet (Oregon) and Trio Libermé (Berlin), and she lives in Corvallis, Oregon, with her husband and two daughters. *Crescendo* is her first book.

AntheaKreston.com
Instagram: @AntheaKreston

www.ingramcontent.com/pod-product-compliance
Lightning Source LLC
Jackson TN
JSHW080713300726
105902JS00001B/1
* 9 7 8 1 5 8 9 8 8 2 1 7 1 *